# THE WORLD'S BEST
# CURRY
# RECIPES

## R. Maheswari Devi

**Food photography** *Yim Chee Peng*

TIMES EDITIONS

ACKNOWLEDGEMENTS

The publishers wish to record their thanks to
Lim's Arts and Crafts
Aw Pottery and
Twin Bird Pte Ltd
for the use of their beautiful tableware

Food photographs by Yim Chee Peng, Culinary Studios
Graphics by Jennifer Chua
Design by Lim Hoon Eng

Text © 1984 Maheswari Devi
Photographs and Graphics © 1984 Times Editions Pte Ltd
Photographs and Graphics © 2000 Times Media Private Limited

First published as
International Curry Cooking
Reprinted 1995
This edition published in 2000

Published by Times Editions
An imprint of Times Media Private Limited
A member of the Times Publishing Group
Times Centre, 1 New Industrial Road
Singapore 536196
Tel: (65) 2848844  Fax: (65) 2854871
Email: te@tpl.com.sg
Online bookstore: http://www.timesone.com.sg/te

Times Subang
Lot 46, Subang Hi-Tech Industrial Park
Batu Tiga, 40000 Shah Alam
Selangor Darul Ehsan, Malaysia
Tel & Fax: (603) 7363517
Email: cchong@tpg.com.my

Printed by Times Offset (M) Sdn Bhd, Malaysia

ISBN 981-232-135-7

# CONTENTS

# PREFACE

In The World's Best Curry Recipes, Maheswari Devi proves herself a gastronome of rare integrity. As its title suggests, the book is remarkably complete and expertly presented. It is more than simply the finest book on curry cuisine. Far ranging in its scope, this first authentic, comprehensive and unique treasury of curry cooking has informative notes on every cooking technique, including the basic grammar of curry cooking, blends of curry powder, methods of introducing ingredients to curries as well as uses and descriptions of herbs, spices and unusual ingredients.

Although curry cooking originated in India, the cooking of curry is no longer confined to the subcontinent. The collection of more than 300 kitchen-tested and easy-to-follow recipes is proof of this. Over the past years, Maheswari Devi's research into how others use spices to cook curry dishes has led her to painstakingly collect recipes from various countries. She has also created many dishes by experimenting with different combinations of spices without sacrificing the essential regional character of each dish. Flavourful, tempting and authentic, these recipes are indispensable for today's discerning cook.

Maheswari Devi, who is widely travelled and has a London Diploma in Hotel Catering, is not new to the cookery scene in Singapore. She has taken part in cookery demonstrations, made television appearances and had her recipes published both locally and abroad. Her previous book, Handy Rice Recipes, was selected as one of the best books published in Singapore in 1971. There are many cookery books on the market today but this book is absolutely gripping in the way a cookery book should be.

*Lau Siew Kheng*

# INTRODUCTION

*"And nearer as they came,*
*a genial savour of certain stews, and roast-meats, and pilaus,*
*Things which in hungry mortals' eyes find favour."*
                                        *LORD BYRON*

Historical Hindu texts reveal that the art of curry cooking originated in India as early as 3600 B.C. and is as old as the Indus Empire. By the fifth century A.D., Sheta Karma's cookbook entitled 'Kheme Sharma' provided the unique treasury of how the Hindu temple priests experimented with spices and herbs to evolve a prized dish called 'Kari' for their Gods. The Hindus like to think cooking curry is a distinctive art form — and a very practical one at that. It is an art that should delight their Gods. Or, as a Hindu saying puts it, a well prepared curry dish should appeal to all the senses. The techniques of this art have been developed and refined over thousands of years.

Curries are eaten and enjoyed throughout the world. Although native to India, many countries have adopted and modified curry cooking techniques because they liked the taste and they had the spices. There are many gastronomes who believe that traditional curry cooking is part of the most sophisticated culinary heritage on Earth. It is infinitely more varied and more extensively used than French or Chinese cuisine, and, in essence, it has become known as the "Salt of the East".

In India, there is a definite curry cookery style, although curries differ with varying climatic and agricultural conditions. People living in the North, in the Himalayan snows, prefer bland curries while in the areas where the weather is hot, people eat curries to cool off. Curry culture has spread throughout the Far Eastern lands, the Middle East, Europe, the West Indies, the Americas and Australasia.

There are many misconceptions about the word "curry". The term usually implies a dish of almost any cooked food in a reheated sauce, flavoured with herbs and seasoned with curry powder or paste prepared in advance. The liquid in which it simmers may be yogurt, coconut milk, sour cream, cow's milk, goat's milk, tamarind juice, tomato juice, vinegar, various broths or just plain water. Lime, lemon or tamarind juice is usually added to any curry just before it is taken off the heat. All dishes that are hot and spicy are not necessarily curries, nor are all curries fiery hot or acrid. Indian food is not just curry and all curry cooking depends on personal measures of spices. Curries can be hot, mild, bland, sour, sweet, dry, pungent, astringent or various combinations of all these flavours to tempt the palate. They can be prepared in a variety of ways. In the West, South America, the Middle East and Europe, meats are served as stews, roasts, barbecue, hamburgers, minced cutlets, puffed spiced pies, and Indian curry spices are used to flavour each dish.

Curries can, if necessary, be prepared the day before. In such cases, it is best to undercook the dish by a few minutes and keep it covered with foil in a freezer or refrigerator. The time used to reheat the dish will bring it to its finished state. The art of curry making lies in the delicate and subtle blending of aromatic spices by which the flavour and texture of the main ingredients are heightened. There are nine basic spices in the Hindu ritual curry powder, but every country, housewife, or chef can evolve a unique, special blend. With its superb mix of fine flavours, curry cooking has a personality of its own, and never before has it been so widely appreciated in the world. Therefore, there is a wonderland of gastronomic colour, aroma, texture, flavour and richness in curries. They are suitable for all climates and temperaments.

I have included a diversity of recipes that should please every taste: hot recipes from Andhra Pradesh and Madras; Straits Chinese recipes; brown-sugar-rich cuisine from Central Java; yogurt-rich cuisine from the Punjab, Sind and Bihar; almond-flavoured foods from Kashmir; bland curries from Britain; mild curries from the Pacific Islands; peanut-rich dishes from Brazil and Africa; vinegar recipes from Goa; fruit juice bases from Iran; and sweet, hot recipes from Burma, Thailand and Indochina.

This book is firmly rooted in the idea that cooking is a craft. Whether preparing traditional or international recipes, an understanding of the basic principles is vital to achieve the smooth efficiency that allows more time for pleasurable, creative cooking.

Much more than just another collection of recipes, The World's Best Curry Recipes includes informative notes on the basic grammar of curry cooking, blends of curry powder and methods of introducing ingredients to curries. The detailed descriptions and what I believe to be sensible and practical advice will give the average cook confidence in attempting new recipes. This, above all, is the object of my book.

*R. Maheswari Devi*

# BASIC GRAMMAR OF CURRY COOKING

### Preparation of Spices

(a) Dry spices: Coriander seeds, sesame seeds, cumin seeds, poppy seeds and dried chillies are generally roasted and then powdered.

(b) Ginger, garlic and onion paste: should be ground but with no water added while grinding.

### Fats and Oils

Most Indian and Pakistani curries are cooked in ghee, clarified butter, cottonseed oil, sesame oil, vegetable oil, mustard oil or coconut oil. Mustard oil is often used in India for cooking fish. Indonesian, Malaysian, Thai, Burmese, Fijian, Straits Chinese curries are cooked in coconut oil and peanut oil.

### Yogurt and Coconut milk

Most Indians, Arabs and Iranians use yogurt to cook meat. Coconut milk is also used in the Southern, Western and Eastern parts of India, Sri Lanka, Maldives, Caribbean Islands, Africa, Pacific Islands and the Far East.

### Nuts

Candlenuts are used in Malaysian and Indonesian curries. They are creamy coloured nuts from the candle-berry tree. Their purpose is to thicken curries with the oil they produce. Indonesian, Malaysian and Brazilian recipes include a sauce using ground peanuts. If candlenuts are not available, use Brazilian nuts or almonds.

### Basic Flavourings

Shrimp paste is used in very small amounts as a flavouring in a variety of Indonesian, Malaysian, Thai, Burmese and Straits Chinese dishes.

The Burmese and Thais use a pungent fish sauce called nam pla. Sri Lankans use Maldive fish in their curries which look every bit as much as bits of dried wood.

### Thickening Agents

To give curry paste more body, ground poppy seeds, gram powder, rice flour, potato and coconut milk can be added. Pounded fenugreek is added to a white curry. Kneaded butter is another excellent ingredient for this purpose; it is made with one tablespoon butter and one tablespoon flour, mixed and pounded together into a smooth paste.

### Tenderising agents

Fruits: Slices of papaya are added to raw meat prior to cooking and removed before the meat is cooked. The leaf of a papaya is added for tenderising meat that is to be grilled.

Lime, tamarind, mango, tomato, belimbing are the mildest of acids used for tenderising meat.

**Curd and Yogurt:** The curd or yogurt is applied to the meat and allowed to remain for sometime.

**Vinegar:** The acetic acid in vinegar helps to soften meat. Vinegar is mixed with the meat and allowed to remain for $1/4 - 1/2$ hour prior to cooking.

### Blending a Good Curry Powder

All spices must be fresh and should be purchased whole. All curry powder, must be cooked before adding it to the other ingredients. In most uses the curry powder should be fried well in a small amount of heated oil.

### Crushing Spices into a Paste

In India and Sri Lanka, the grinding is done with a stone roller and a rough, stone base. The traditional Indian method of preparing curry powder is to pulverise all the spices in a wooden mortar with a steel-rimmed wooden pestle. Small mortars and pestles are used to crush betel-nuts. These methods are found in all curry producing regions.

An equally acceptable method of making the paste is to combine all the ingredients with a little coconut milk, water or oil to be used in simmering or sauteeing in an electric liquidiser, and liquidise it at high speed until well mixed.

### How to Saute Curry Paste

Place the oil in a pan and when warm, add the paste. Saute for a minute or two. Stir constantly with a wooden spoon to prevent any burning.

Make sure that you add no extra oil when you put the liquidised paste into a heated pan on the stove. The oil you have used in the liquidiser will produce the necessary frying result.

## The Use of Dried Chillies for Sambal
Put dried chillies into a small amount of water and allow to soak for a couple of minutes. Drain. Pound or liquidise.

## How to Roast Shrimp Paste
Wrap the shrimp paste in foil and roast it in a pan on top of the stove for a minute or two. Then remove the foil wrapper and use as required. Alternatively, it can either be roasted crumbled in a heated pan or pressed into a wafer and toasted.

## The Use of Ghee
Melt the ghee on a very low heat until it dissolves, strain. Ghee does not burn and does not splutter.

## Preparing Lentils
Soak them in water and cover for 4 hours or more until they become soft enough to mix with the other ingredients. Then wash and remove loose skin.

## How to make Tamarind juice
Soak a tablespoon of tamarind concentrate or paste in 125 ml water; then squeeze and press it, so that the water becomes thick and brown. Strain.

## Making Fried Onion Flakes
Slice onions very thinly crosswise. Fry in hot oil, turning so that they brown evenly. When brown, remove and drain on paper towels. It is used for garnishing.

## Crushing Garlic for Curries
Peel the cloves. Smash them with a flat side of a cleaver, and chop roughly with the blunt edge.

## A Substitute for Indonesian Soya Sauce
Combine 4 tablespoons ordinary soya sauce with five tablespoons dark corn syrup.

## How to fry Pappadum and Krupuk
Any kind of pappadum or lentil wafer and krupuk or shrimp wafer is cooked in the following manner.
Heat oil until hot but not smoking. Place 1 or 2 pieces into the hot oil. Keep it in motion to allow the pieces to swell to their full size. Remove and drain on absorbent papers. The wafer, which will be very crisp, can be served immediately or can be stored in an air tight container.

## Preparing Yogurt
Yogurt is made with the milk from cows, sheep, goats and buffaloes.
Bring 500 ml milk to a boil, reduce heat and simmer for a minute. Turn off the heat and let the milk cool. Add two tablespoons of previously made yogurt to the boiled milk from which the yogurt is to be made. Mix well until smooth.

Let stand for 3 hours.

## How to make Curd
Bring 500 ml fresh milk to a boil and remove. While still warm, add one tablespoon lime juice. Let the mixture stand covered in a warm room for 24 hours.

## Making Panir Cottage Cheese
Bring 500 ml milk to a boil, then add a tablespoon lime juice. Mix well. When lumps are formed strain through a fine cloth to press out the whey.
The whey or excess watery substance can be use in curries.

## Preparing Thick Coconut Milk
1) Cover the grated coconut with cold or hot water.
2) Let it steep well until cool enough to handle, then knead with your hands until the liquid is milky.
3) Squeeze out the milk into a bowl through a fine strainer or cloth.

## Preparing Thin Coconut Milk
Milk from the second extraction is made by repeating the extraction procedure again and again by using the same grated coconut that was used for extracting the thick coconut milk.

## Milk from Desiccated Coconut
1. Cover it with hot water. Allow coconut to soak for twenty minutes.
2. Knead with your hands until the liquid is milky.
3. Squeeze out the milk into a bowl through a fine strainer.

If you have an electric liquidiser, transfer the coconut mixture to it.

## Ground Coconut
Grind or liquidise the coconut into a paste.

## Coconut Cream
There are a number of commercial coconut cream preparations. Coconut cream is obtained by squeezing the grated coconut without adding water.

90 ml coconut cream = 240 ml thick coconut milk
30 ml coconut cream = 240 ml thin coconut milk

When a recipe specifies "coconut milk", you can use 85 ml thick coconut milk and 165 ml thin coconut milk.

## How to Roast Coconut
1. Heat a pan.
2. Add grated coconut and stir all the while until the desired colour is obtained.

### How to Store Curries

Refrigerate curries in a covered container. For longer storage wrap in moisture/vapourproof material and keep in freezer.

### Recooking Frozen Curries

Re-heat food in original dish — it can be put frozen into the oven or it can be thawed and then re-heated thoroughly.

### How to cook Rice

(1) Place rice in strainer and rinse thoroughly in cold running water. Drain.
(2) Place one cup of long grain rice with two cups of water.
(3) Bring to the boil over a high flame (about five minutes).
(4) Turn flame to low and allow to simmer for twenty minutes until dry.
(5) Turn off flame. Stir well while rice is still hot so it will be flaky and the grains separate.

### How to serve Rice

To serve, mound the rice in the centre of a platter and arrange the curries, sambals, pickle, chutney, chips, pappadums or krupuk around the rice. Decorate with slices of hard-boiled eggs, tomato wedges and cucumber slices.

### Planning a Menu

(1) The best way is to start with a simple balanced diet which would consist of rice; meat, fish or poultry; egg; vegetable; a sambal; pickle and soup, yogurt or spiced broths.
(2) Try to choose dishes that are cooked by different methods.

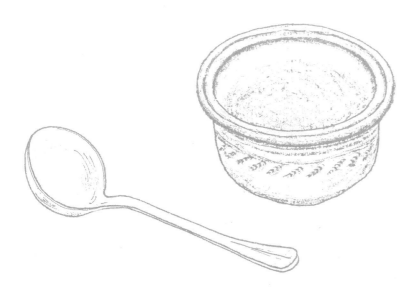

# METHODS OF CURRY COOKING

## Boiling
In boiling, the food is cooked in some liquid such as water, yogurt, sour cream, goats' milk, cow's milk, stock or brine.

## Steaming
Steaming is cooking by moist heat, vapour or steam given out from boiling water.

## Stewing
Stewing is cooking by moist heat over a low flame (75°C – 90°C) in a minimum quantity of liquid over a long period of time. Sufficient water is added to the food from the start.

## Shallow-Frying
Using enough oil to cover the bottom of the frying pan, the food is spread evenly in the pan and allowed to fry slowly for a few minutes.

## Stir Frying
This is a technique of frying foods over a high flame, stirring continuously and vigorously for the duration of cooking, which is usually a few minutes. A small amount of oil is used and it is heated before the other ingredients are added.

## Sauteeing
This is the cooking of food in a small quantity of very hot oil in which the ingredients are tossed until browned or cooked.

## Braising
Food is cooked at a low temperature in a small amount of liquid in a covered pot until done.

## Deep Frying
In this method of cooking the food is completely covered with hot oil.

## Simmering
It is a continuation of the boiling process carried on at a lower temperature than that of the boiling process. This is above stewing point.

## Roasting
The food prepared in this manner develop very delicate flavours and also retains most of its moisture. This is due to the heat penetration being gradual and indirect. In Sri Lanka, curry powders or spices are roasted in a pan without any oil or liquid to give flavour.

## Basting
Basting is the pouring of liquid every 15 – 20 minutes over meat that is being roasted or baked. The liquid may be oil, water or stock.

## Grilling or Broiling
The element of the grill must always be pre-heated before the food is placed over or under the grill. The food should be allowed to marinade or sufficient oil be applied prior to grilling to retain the moisture of the food.

## Baking
The oven should always be pre-heated. Baking of egg-plants in India or Sri Lanka is usually done in hot ash or over live coals.

## Charcoal Cooking
Any of the basic methods — baking, broiling, grilling, frying, boiling or steaming can be used over hot charcoal.

# METHODS OF INTRODUCING INGREDIENTS TO CURRIES

It must be remembered that more or less the same basic ingredients are used for all curries. Different flavours are obtained by combining them in different proportions and also by introducing them to the main ingredients in different ways.

(1) In this method the condiments used are all mixed with the raw food. Thin coconut milk or thick coconut milk or yogurt is added to the curry, brought to the boil and allowed to simmer until done.

(2) All the ingredients such as condiments, spices and seasonings are mixed and then cooked in a little oil to bring out the flavour of the spice mixture. Then, the necessary coconut milk or yogurt is added.

(3) The spices and condiments are added to a very small quantity of oil and fried until an aroma is obtained. Thereafter meat, fish or vegetables are added and fried for a few minutes. Then coconut milk or yogurt is added.

(4) The curry powder is roasted in a heated pan for a few minutes. Then it is added to meat, poultry, fish, vegetables or lentils. Coconut milk or yogurt is added.

(5) In this method the whole condiments and spices are powdered and ground prior to immediate use.

(6) Bring the coconut milk very slowly to a simmer and when the mixture becomes bubbly, add the ground spices and seasonings. It is then added to the vegetables or lentils.

(7) Mix all the spices and yogurt and simmer in boiling water for an hour. Then seal the mixture in a sterilised jar. Serve with rice or chicken.

(8) Small pieces of meat or fish are marinated in a spice mixture, then grilled, skewered or braised.

# TERMS TO KNOW

**Blend**
To mix thoroughly or to grind finely in an electric blender or liquidizer.

**Chop**
Cut into uneven pieces with a knife or cleaver.

**Squeeze**
Press to extract juice.

**Cube**
Cut into 1 cm cubes or larger.

**Dice**
Cut into small cubes

**Grate**
Rub into tiny particles using a grater.

**Grind**
To crush into fine, medium or coarse particles.

**Julienne**
Cut into match-like sticks.

**Mince**
Cut into very fine pieces.

**Pare**
Cut off outside covering with a knife.

**Peel**
Strip off outside covering.

**Pound**
To finely grind to a paste or powder with a mortar and pestle.

**Shred**
Cut into thin pieces or to grate.

**Sliver**
Cut into thin long pieces

# INGREDIENTS

**Allspice**
Known as Jamaica pepper, it is small, hard, black and resembles peppercorn. It has the blended flavour of cloves, nutmeg and cinnamon and is used for flavouring and in pickles, relishes, sauces, stews and soups. Hindus use it mainly in many of their curry powders.

**Aniseed (Sweet Cummin)**
A small, dried seed it has a strong liquorice flavour. The seeds are roasted before pounding and grinding.

**Asafoetida**
Gum resin obtained from the roots and rhizome of ferula foetida. Used as a condiment in Southern and Western India.

**Basil**
An aromatic herb whose flavour resembles that of sweet cloves. It is used in soups, sauces, grilled fish, vegetables and egg dishes.

**Bay Leaves**
A herb. Available fresh, dried and powdered. It is added to stews and curries.

**Bean Curd**
Made from pureed soya beans, it is available in many consistencies: firm, soft and dried.

**Candlenuts**
They are heart-shaped and cream coloured. Ground candlenuts thicken sauces and are vital to Malaysian and Indonesian cooking.

**Capsicum**
Sweet pepper or Bell pepper. It is available in various sizes and in red, yellow and green.

**Caraway Seeds**
Black seeds similar to anise in appearance. An important addition to curry powders and used for flavouring of pastries, bread, soups and pickles.

**Cardamom**
These are small pods known as the seed of Paradise. Can be used whole, ground or crushed. Gives delicate flavour and aroma.

**Cayenne Pepper**
Darker in colour than paprika. Very hot and pungent.

**Chilli**
There are many varieties of this vegetable. Can be green, yellow, purple or red. Ripe chillies are usually red and the seeds have a fiery pungency. Kashmiri chillies are of a fine flavour and not very hot.

**Chives**
Small onion-like green sprouts. They add colour and flavour to egg dishes, salads, soups and potato dishes.

**Cinnamon**
Outer bark of the cinnamon tree. Can be added whole, ground or crushed to curries, pickles, rice, drinks, pies, puddings and pastries. It has a pleasing fragrant odour and a sweet aromatic taste.

**Citronella Grass**
Known also as lemon grass it has a pungent lemony fragrance. Use only the root (10 – 15 cm), discarding the tough leaves. Used in Malaysian, Ceylonese, Indonesian and Thai dishes.

**Cloves**
Dried unopened buds of a tropical tree of the myrtle family. Highly aromatic, it is available whole or in powdered form. Improves pickles, sauces and pilaus.

**Coriander Seeds**
Small, yellowish seeds with a sweet lemon flavour.

**Coriander Leaves**
Used as a garnish and ingredient in curries. Fresh leaves are used by Thais and Indians.

## Curry Leaves
Varieties of curry leaves have an aromatic flavour and give fragrance to curries.

## Drumsticks
A colloquial Indian name for the long pods of the horse radish tree.

## Fennel Seed
Pungent sweet, aromatic smell and tastes like aniseed. Used extensively in Sri Lanka and Scandinavian cooking.

## Fenugreek Seeds
Yellowish brown seeds of the plant of the pea family. Used to flavour and thicken curries.

## Fish Sauce
The characteristic and distinctive flavour of Thai and Burmese curries come from one of the three ingredients: Coriander leaves, coriander root and fish sauce. Fish sauce is made from salted fish that is steamed, roasted or fried.

## Five Spice Powder
Fragrant, reddish brown spice mixture that combines star anise, fennel, cinnamon, clove and peppercorns. Used by Chinese.

## Galangal
Brown root with white flesh similar in appearance to ginger. Grows throughout South East Asia.

## Garam Masala
This consists of equal amounts of cardamons, cinnamon, cloves and cumin ground to a powder. Pungent, with a piercing flavour, it is used in vegetable and meat curries.

## Gherkins
These are very small sweet or sour pickled cucumbers.

## Ginger
The root of the ginger plant. It is used in spicing curries and as a condiment.

## Jaggery
Brown sugar made from the saps of various palms.

## Lemon Grass
See Citronella grass.

## Limes
Small, oval or round citrus fruits but smaller than lemons.

## Lime Leaf
Fragrant leaf of the citrus family known as daun limau perut. Adds an orange tint to food. Used by Indonesians.

## Mace
Called the "pound cake spice" and comes from the peach-like fruit similar to nutmeg. Adds flavour to curries. pickles, fish sauce and light fruit cakes.

## Maldive Fish
Dried fish from the Maldive Islands. A great delicacy in Sri Lanka and is used in most curries.

## Mint
Fragrant herb. Used in chutneys or sambals. Much used in Indian cooking.

## Mustard
Tiny black or yellow seeds. Used in pickles, chutneys, garnishing and curry powders. Ground seeds become dry mustard.

## Nutmeg
Large seed of a peach-like evergreen tree used to flavour curries, puddings and soups. Interchangeable with mace in recipes.

## Onion
Small reddish onions give a rich flavour in curries, sambals, pickles and chutneys. Used extensively by Northern Sri Lankans in all curries. Large onions are known as Bombay or Spanish onions.

## Paprika
These are ground seeds of sweet red pepper. There are two kinds of paprika: Spanish paprika is slightly mild in flavour and has a bright red colour; Hungarian paprika is darker in colour and more pungent in flavour.

## Parsley
It is a delicate herb. The leaves are used as a garnish or to flavour other foods. It is used in soups, salads, stuffing, stews, sauces, potatoes and vegetable dishes.

## Peppercorns
There are black and white peppercorns. Black peppercorns have a distinctive penetrating aromatic odour but the white is not so pungent.

## Pickling Spice
It consists of peppercorns, chillies and cloves.

## Poppy Seeds
Nutlike flavour with a pleasant and agreeable texture. A favourite addition to curry powder blends.

## Saffron
Filaments of the rarest and most exotic of spice plants. Gives a rich flavour and colour.

### Screwpine Leaf
Long, dark green leaf of the pandanus palm.

### Sesame Seeds
Yields sesame oil. It has a pleasing nut flavour.

### Shallots
Shallots are of the green onion family but have a bulb that consists of several cloves similar to the garlic bulb.

### Shrimp Paste
This is made from fermented prawns or shrimps, salted and pounded. Soft pink or dark coloured and mushy or hard, it is very pungent. Vital to Thai, Malay, Indonesian and Burmese cooking.

### Soya Sauce
Made from soya bean, grain, malt, yeast and salt. The Javanese variety is sweet. Light soya sauce is used in cooking. Vital to Indonesian, Chinese and Japanese cooking.

### Sweet Cumin
Referred to as big or white cumin.

### Tamarind
The Persian name for this is Tamar-i-Hind, which means "Date of India". It is used in curries. Tamarind has a distinct sour taste.

### Turmeric
This spice has a sweet flavour and gives a brilliant colour to food.

# UTENSILS

### Charcoal Stove
The basic traditional equipment in an average Asian kitchen is the charcoal stove.

### Earthernware Curry Pot
This is the traditional Indian vessel which retains the flavour of curries.

### Kwali or Wok
It is the cooking pan with a rounded bottom and gently sloping sides. The Wok is the basin kitchen utensil in South East Asia and is used as a deep-fryer, saucepan, frying pan, saute-pan and braising pan. A small amount of oil is required and the temperature can be regulated.

### Grater
Used for grating coconut, carrot and the like.

### Grinding Base and Roller
Rectangular shaped piece of granite on which spices are ground with a granite roller. The electric liquidiser is a successful substitute.

### Mortar and Pestle
These are made of granite and used for pounding condiments and sambals.

### Thali
A round silver or stainless steel salver used as a serving plate.

# SUPPLIERS

The leading brand in the English market is undoubtedly "Veerasamy curry powder" (mild), (hot) made by the renowned Indian chef of the popular Indian restaurant in Regent Street, London. English women are more familiar with this brand which can be found in the food departments of Harrods, Selfridges, Civil Service Stores in the Strand, Tesco supermarkets, Evans and all Indian grocery shops.

"Conimex" and "Runel" brand curry powders are very good choices for Indonesian, Malaysian, Thai and Burmese curries.

Following is a list of stores where spices can be purchased.

(1) G.B. Cortney & Co Pte Ltd,
    Suite 12, 171, Fitzery Street, St. Hild,
    Melbourne, Australia.

(2) Netter & Co,
    18, Rue Pierre, Juerin,
    Paris, France.

(3) Otte R.E. Miller,
    8 – 10, Neue Groningerstrasse, Namasahaus,
    Hamburg, Germany.

(4) Gourmets Bazar,
    lue, 3, Purdy Avenue, Rye,
    New York.

(5) Pirry's Dixieland Market,
    1108 Pharmacy Avenue,
    Ontario, Canada.

Many ingredients used in curries are readily available in local food markets or in ethnic food markets or shops.

# EASY REFERENCES

## LIST OF ABBREVIATIONS

| | | |
|---|---|---|
| tsp | ................................. | teaspoon |
| tbsp | ................................. | tablespoon |
| g | ................................. | gramme |
| kg | ................................. | kilogram |
| ml | ................................. | millilitre |
| cm | ................................. | centimetre |

## TEMPERATURE CHART
Slow oven: 121° – 149°C (250° – 300°F)
Moderate oven: 149° – 177°C (300° – 350°F)
Hot oven: 177° – 204°C (350° – 400°F)
Quick oven: 204° – 232°C (400° –450°F)
Very Quick oven: 232° – 260°C (450° – 500°F)

## TEMPERATURE CHART
(for frying oil process)

| | |
|---|---|
| Cutlets ................................. | 175°C (350°F) |
| Fried fish ................................. | 175°C (350°F) |
| Fritters (banana etc) ................... | 175°C (350°F) |
| Ladies finger and eggplants ......... | 180°C (360°F) |
| Krupuk/pappadam ...................... | 190°C (370°F) |
| Re-heated food (second frying) ...... | 195°C (380°F) |
| Raw starchy food (chips) ............. | 170°C (340°F) |

## WEIGHTS AND MEASURES
Note: conversions are approximate only.

| | | | |
|---|---|---|---|
| 1 tsp .............. | 1/6 oz .............. | 5 ml .............. | 5 g |
| 1 tbsp .............. | ½ oz .............. | 15 ml .............. | 15 g |
| 1 cup .............. | 8 ozs .............. | 250 ml .............. | 225 g |

| | |
|---|---|
| 1 oz ................................. | 30 g |
| 8 ozs ................................. | 225 g |
| 16 ozs ................................. | 456 g |
| 1 oz ................................. | 30 ml |

## HOME MEASURES
For flour, sugar, rice, sago and dried fruits, etc

| | |
|---|---|
| ⅛ tsp ................................. | a pinch |
| 1 tsp sugar ................................. | 5 g |
| 1 tbsp rice flour ................................. | 9 g |
| 1 tbsp gram flour ................................. | 8 g |
| 1 piece fresh turmeric ............ | 2 cm x 1 cm thick |
| 1 piece dried shrimp paste ......... | 5 cm x 2.5 cm |
| 1 slice galangal ................. | .32 cm thick |

## POWDERED CURRY STUFFS

| | |
|---|---|
| 1 tsp coriander seeds ................. | 4 g |
| 1 tsp ginger powder ................... | 2 g |
| 1 tsp chilli powder ..................... | 2 g |
| 1 tbsp coriander powder ............. | 10 g |
| 1 tbsp ghee/butter ..................... | 20 g |

## LIQUIDS

| | | | |
|---|---|---|---|
| 1 cup .............. | ¼ l .............. | 250 ml .............. | ½ pint |
| 2 cups .............. | ½ l .............. | 500 ml .............. | 1 pint |
| 4⅓ cups ......... | 1 l .............. | 1000 ml .............. | 1 quart, 2 ozs |

*British measure

# Curry Powder Blends

*"The discovery of a new dish does more for the happiness of man than the discovery of a star."*

— BRILLAT-SAVARIN

# Hints For Beginners

All spices must be fresh and purchased whole. Dry spices: coriander seeds, sesame seeds, cumin seeds, poppy seeds and chillies are generally roasted and then powdered or liquidised (ground in a blender).

Curry powders are used for preparing meat, seafood, eggs, poultry and vegetables or lentils. They are not used in seasoning, pickles, or sprinkled on potato chips, fried nuts and sliced tomatoes. For these chilli powder is used. The curry powders which contain fennel seeds can be used for any South East Asian or Sri Lanka curry. Fennel seed is never an ingredient of Indian, Pakistani, or Bangladesh curry powder. Always store curry powders in dry air tight containers.

# Hindu Ritual or Basic Blend
*(A Very Mild Blend for Vegetables)*

240 g coriander seeds
110 g cumin seeds
 10 g turmeric
 10 g dried ginger root
  2 cardamom pods
  2 dried red chillies
  7 peppercorns
  5 g mustard seeds
 60 g saffron

---

METHOD

1. Clean, wash, and dry the spices in the sun.
2. Then roast in a dry pan until fragrant.
3. Liquidise or pound to a fine powder.
4. Cool well. Then store in air tight container. This curry powder will keep for 4 months or longer if untouched by damp fingers or spoons.

# Jaffna Vegetable/Lentils Curry Powder
*(A Mildly-hot Blend)*

120 g coriander seeds
 60 g dried chillies
 10 g fenugreek seeds
  1 sprig curry leaves
 30 g black peppercorns
 30 g cumin seeds
  5 cm piece turmeric

---

METHOD

1. Clean, wash and then sun-dry the spices for 2 or 3 days.
2. Roast the spices and curry leaves over a uniform heat until very hot to the touch.
3. Liquidise or pound and sieve. Cool well. Then store in air tight containers.

**Note:**
Add 240 g dried chillies instead of 60 g dried chillies for a hot blend.

# Sri Lankan Sinhalese Vegetable Curry Powder
*(A Mild Blend)*

120 g coriander seeds
 90 g cumin seeds
 60 g coconut, dried
 60 g sweet cumin seeds
 60 g fenugreek seeds
 15 g rice
 ¼ tsp turmeric powder

---

METHOD

1. Clean, dry the spices or roast in the pan until very hot to the touch.
2. Liquidise the coriander seeds, cumin seeds, sweet cumin seeds, fenugreek seeds, rice and coconut. Mix thoroughly. Cool well.
3. Now add the turmeric powder, mix well. Store in air tight containers.

**Note:**
This curry powder can be used for any South East Asian curry.

# Indian Vegetable Curry Powder
*(A Fairly Mild Blend)*

240 g coriander seeds
240 g cumin seeds
 40 g turmeric
 75 g dried ginger root
 15 g mustard seeds
  2 cardamom pods
  5 peppercorns
  2 dried chillies

## METHOD

1. Roast the cleaned spices separately until they become very hot to the touch.
2. Now mix the spices and liquidise or pound. Sift through a fairly fine sieve.
3. Cool well. Store in air tight container.

# Hindu Vegetarian Curry Powder

255 g dried chillies
255 g coriander seeds
 42 g black peppercorns
 45 g cumin seeds
 45 g fenugreek seeds
 42 g mustard seeds

## METHOD

1. Sun dry the above ingredients separately until crisp and warm.
2. Now, roast them all separately over a uniform heat. Roast the chillies in a little ghee.
3. Pound or liquidise to a fine powder. Sift. Cool well. Store.

## Note:

This curry has a vegetarian flavour of its own. Omit the chillies and it would give a basic mild blend. It is used for all kinds of vegetables, lentils and vegetable pilaus.

# Indian Sambhar Curry Powder
*(A Hot Blend for Vegetables)*

200 g dried red chillies
 50 g yellow split lentils
 20 g fenugreek seeds
  2 tsps turmeric powder
100 g coriander seeds
 12 g cumin seeds
 12 g mustard seeds

## METHOD

1. Roast the spices individually, then powder them.
2. Mix and store in an air tight jar till required.

## Note:

Use 2 tbsp. of Sambhar powder for 1½ litres water and 450 g vegetables. It will keep for 6 months or more.

# Indian Meat Curry Powder
*(A Mild Blend)*

450 g coriander seeds
 75 g black peppercorns
120 g cumin seeds
  5 cm stick cinnamon
  4 cloves
112 g turmeric
 60 g fenugreek seeds
(garam masala to be added)
  5 cardamom pods
  4 cm piece fresh ginger (paste)

## METHOD

1. Roast the cleaned spices and liquidise or pound the spices separately.
2. Mix the spices thoroughly. Cool well. Store in air tight container.

## Note:

Grind the skinned ginger into a paste before adding to the other spices when cooking. Indian curries are sprinkled with garam masala just before removing pot from the fire. Cinnamon, cardamon pods and cloves should be omitted if curries are sprinkled with garam masala.

# Indian Tandoori Curry Powder
*(A Mild Blend)*

10 g coriander seeds
10 g cumin seeds
10 g fresh ginger
or 5 g dry ginger powder
 3 g chilli powder
 5 g turmeric powder
 5 g cardamom powder
 5 g garlic powder
 5 g black peppercorns

## METHOD

1. Roast and pound or liquidise coriander seeds, cumin seeds, black peppercorns.
2. Mix pounded ingredients with chilli powder, turmeric powder, cardamom powder, garlic powder and ginger powder. Store in an air tight container.

## Note:

If using fresh ginger, add only during cooking.

# South East Asian Meat Curry Powder
*(A Hot Blend)*

225 g coriander seeds
125 g dried chillies
 60 g cumin seeds
  4 cloves
  5 cm piece cinnamon
 30 g peppercorns
 30 g turmeric
 60 g fennel seeds
  3 cardamom pods

### METHOD

1. Clean and wash the spices and dry in the sun or roast them in a dry pan.
2. Liquidise or pound them. Cool well. Store the liquidised powder in air tight container.

**Note:**
Lemon grass, galangal, candlenuts and shrimp paste are to be added during cooking.

# Indian Rasam Curry Powder
*(A Spicy Blend for Broths)*

300 g coriander seeds
 75 g black peppercorns
 10 g mustard seeds
 50 g dried red chillies
 50 g cumin seeds
  1 sprig curry leaves

### METHOD

1. Roast the spices separately in a dry pan and cool.
2. Liquidise or pound each spice separately into a coarse powder.
3. The roasted curry leaves should not be liquidised or pounded.
4. Mix all the spices and curry leaves and store in an air tight container.

**Note:**
One tablespoon of Rasam powder is needed for every 1¼ litres of lentil soup, broth or water.

# Sri Lanka Sinhalese Meat Curry Powder
*(A Hot Blend)*

225 g coriander seeds
125 g black peppercorns
  3 cardamon pods
  5 cm stick cinnamon
lemon grass (optional)
 60 g fennel seeds
 60 g cumin seeds
  5 cloves
  5 cm piece fresh turmeric

### METHOD

1. Roast the spices separately and liquidise or pound them.
2. Sift and cool. Store in an air tight container.

# Jaffna Meat Curry Powder
*(A Mildly-hot Blend)*

240 g coriander seeds
112 g dried chillies
 30 g turmeric powder
garam masala
 90 g cumin seeds
 30 g poppy seeds
 45 g peppercorns

### METHOD

1. Clean, wash and dry or roast until very hot to the touch.
2. Liquidise or pound. Sift. Cool well. Store in an air tight container.

**Note:**
Fresh ginger is to be added only during cooking.

*Different Blends of Curry Powders.*

# South East Asian Seafood Curry Powder
*(A Mildly-hot Blend)*

220 g coriander seeds
100 g dried chillies
  60 g cumin seeds
  30 g turmeric
  25 g peppercorns
  60 g fennel seeds
   1 tsp nutmeg powder

### METHOD

1. Clean, roast the spices in a dry pan and pound or liquidise them to a fine powder. Cardamom powder is an ingredient in some Indonesian seafood recipes. Cinnamon powder is an ingredient in most Thai recipes.
2. Mix thoroughly with nutmeg powder. Store in air tight container.

**Note:**
Cardamom, candlenuts, galangal, cinnamon, lemon grass and shrimp paste to be added during cooking.

# Indian Mixed Spices

30 g black mustard seeds
30 g cumin seeds
15 g fennel seeds
15 g caraway seeds
15 g fenugreek seeds

### METHOD

Roast and combine the five spices and store in an air tight container. Use as directed.

# Sri Lanka Seafood Curry Powder
*(A Hot Blend)*

300 g dried chillies
150 g coriander seeds
  60 g cumin seeds
pinch of fennel seeds
  15 g turmeric powder
  35 g peppercorns
  10 g fenugreek seeds

### METHOD

Roast and pound or liquidise the spices. Cool well. Store in an air tight container.

# Indian Seafood/Egg Curry Powder
*(Fairly Hot Blend)*

120 g coriander seeds
  30 g cumin seeds
  10 g garlic powder
  10 g turmeric
  30 g black peppercorns
  30 g mustard seeds (optional)
  15 dried chillies

### METHOD

Roast, pound or liquidise the spices. Cool. Then store in an air tight container.

**Note:**
Omit dried chillies if you require a mild blend.

# Chinese Five-Spice Mixture Curry Powder

100 g star anise
100 g anise
100 g fennel
100 g cinnamon
100 g cloves

### METHOD

Mix together equal quantities of the five spices and grind to a fine powder. Store in an air tight container. Use in meat, fish, vegetable and poultry recipes as directed.

# Garam Masala and Fragrant Spice Powders

Garam masala and fragrant spice powders are fragrant and strong. A pinch should be added at the end of the cooking time so that its delicate flavour is retained. The spices used are variable.

To prepare the following blends, grind the spices coarsely fine. Store in an air tight jar.

## Jaffna Fragrant Spice Powder
*(Meat Blend)*

90 g cumin seeds
45 g cloves
40 g cinnamon
10 cardamom pods

This fragrant spice powder is sprinkled on vegetable curries too.

## Indian Garam Masala
*(Meat Blend)*

90 g black peppercorns
90 g coriander seeds
 5 cardamom pods
30 g cinnamon
30 g cloves

## Sri Lanka Sinhalese Fragrant Spice Powder
*(Vegetable Blend)*

30 g cumin seeds
 6 cardamom pods
 4 coriander seeds
30 g fennel seeds
 1 clove
 2 cm stick cinnamon

## Indian Garam Masala
*(Vegetable Blend)*

30 g cumin seeds
16 cloves
15 black peppercorns
 6 cardamom pods

# Curry Pastes

*"Better is a dinner of herbs where love is, than a stalled ox and
hatred therewith."*

(Proverbs XV 17)

# Note on Curry Pastes

A curry of any variety should be an aromatic mixture of freshly ground herbs and spices. There are several main categories of pastes.

# Thai Green Curry Paste for Poultry
*(A Very Hot Blend)*

10 red chillies, minced
 2 stalks lemon grass, chopped
 1 large onion, minced
10 g coriander roots
12 peppercorns
 1 tsp galangal powder
 2 tbsp garlic, minced
 1 tsp salt
 1 tsp coriander seeds
 1 tsp caraway seeds
 3 cloves
 1 nutmeg
 1 tsp lime rind, dried, soaked
 1 tsp powdered ginger
 1 tsp shrimp paste
3½ tbsps oil

---

METHOD

1.  Liquidise the dry spices, then add the other ingredients including the oil to a smooth paste.

Note:
This paste will keep for at least 1 month in an air tight container in a refrigerator.

# Indian Korma Curry Paste for Poultry
*(A Mild Blend)*

250 ml yogurt
 3 green chillies, minced
 1 tsp cinnamon powder
 1 tsp curry powder for meat
 2 tsps almonds, ground
 1 tsp turmeric, ground
 1 tsp ginger, ground
 1 tsp cardamom powder
 2 tsps poppy seeds, ground
½ tsp black pepper, ground

---

METHOD

1.  The spices should be freshly ground or powdered. Mix all the ingredients in the top part of a boiler. Simmer over boiling water for an hour until mixture loses its raw spice flavour.
2.  Seal the Korma Curry paste in a sterilised jar.

# Indian Vindaloo Paste for Poultry, Meat, Eggs
*(A Hot Blend)*

10 fresh chillies
 6 cloves garlic
 2 cm piece ginger
50 ml vinegar (for grinding)
 2 tsps cumin seeds
 1 tbsp coriander seeds
½ tsp mustard seeds
Oil
 1 tsp sugar

---

METHOD

1.  Combine all the ingredients. Liquidise or pound to make a paste using vinegar.
2.  Heat oil, fry the ground ingredients. Keep in an air tight jar.

# Indonesian Curry Paste for Chicken Livers
*(A Hot Blend)*

FOR ½ KILOGRAM LIVERS
15 dried chillies
 7 cloves garlic
 1 cm piece turmeric
 1 stalk lemon grass
 8 small onions
 5 candlenuts
 2 slices galangal
 1 tbsp coriander seeds
 1 tsp shrimp paste, roasted
 1 tsp sugar

---

METHOD

1.  Pound all the ingredients together into a smooth paste with a little water.

# Indonesian Curry Paste for Chicken
*( A Mild Blend)*

FOR 1 KILOGRAM CHICKEN
5 small onions
3 cloves garlic
4 candlenuts
2 tsps galangal powder
2 tbsp oil
1 tsp chilli powder
2 tsps coriander powder
2 tsps cumin powder
½ tsp shrimp paste

## METHOD
1. Liquidise or pound all the ingredients into a smooth paste.
2. Saute the paste in heated oil. Make sure it does not burn.

# Indonesian Curry Paste For Fried Rice
*(A Mildly-hot Blend)*

FOR 450 g COOKED RICE
9 red chillies
8 cloves garlic
10 small onions
1 tbsp oil
1 tbsp coriander seeds
1 tsp shrimp paste
1 tsp sugar
2 tbsps Javanese soya sauce

## METHOD
1. Pound all the spices and sugar to a coarse fine paste.
2. Heat a tablespoon oil, fry the pounded ingredients until light brown.
3. Add sauce and mix well. Use as required.

# Indian Curry Paste for Pilau Rice
*(A Mildly-hot Blend)*

FOR 1 KILOGRAM LONG GRAIN RICE
300 g small onions, sliced
225 g ghee
2 bay leaves
4 cm stick cinnamon
2 cloves
3 cardamom pods
½ tsp turmeric powder
2¼ tsps cumin seeds
½ tsp cinnamon powder
½ tsp chilli powder
½ tsp cardamom powder

## METHOD
1. Pound all the ground ingredients together with cumin seeds.
2. Heat ghee, fry onions until brown. Remove.
3. Fry powdered spices, whole spices and bay leaves. Add rice and fry till it turns light brown.
4. Cook rice as required.

# Iraqi Curry Paste for Pickles

350 g coriander seeds, roasted, powdered
120 g dry mustard
2 cloves garlic
1 whole nutmeg, grated
125 ml vinegar
¼ tsp black pepper, ground
¼ tsp ground ginger
½ tsp sugar
½ tsp turmeric, ground
½ tsp chilli powder

## METHOD
1. Combine the spices and sugar and fry in heated oil.
2. Add vinegar, stir well. Then add garlic.
3. When the curry paste begins to thicken, remove and cool well.
4. Store in an air tight jar and use it after 3 days.

Note:
Use it for spicing pickles.

*A Variety of Curry Pastes (Overleaf).*

# Thai Curry Paste for Flavouring/Garnishing

10 dried chillies, slit
 5 cloves garlic, chopped
 5 small onions, chopped
 1 tbsp fish sauce
 1 tbsp sugar
2¼ tbsps shrimp powder
 1 tbsp oil

### METHOD

1. Roast the chillies, onions and garlic for 2 minutes in a foil.
2. Allow to cool, then pound to a paste.
3. Heat oil, fry the paste until brown. Add shrimp powder, sugar and fish sauce, stirring well. Refrigerate the paste in a sealed jar.

# Indian Curry Paste for Fried Vegetables
*(A Mild Blend)*

FOR ½ KILOGRAM OF ANY FRIED VEGETABLE
70 g almond kernels
35 g coriander seeds
10 cardamom pods
25 g cinnamon powder
60 g fresh ginger
 5 g cumin seeds
curd (to taste)

### METHOD

1. Grind or liquidise all the ingredients and add it to the curd.
2. Heat it before using it with vegetables such as eggplants fried in oil.

# Jaffna Curry Paste for Lentils/Green Vegetables
*(A Mild Blend)*

FOR ¼ KILOGRAM LENTILS/GREEN VEGETABLES
100 g grated coconut
 3 cloves garlic
 10 peppercorns
 2 dried chillies

### METHOD

1. Liquidise or grind the coconut, garlic, dried chillies and peppercorns to a fine paste.
2. Add to the nearly cooked lentils or vegetables.

# Malay Curry Paste for Vegetables
*(A Mildly-hot Blend)*

FOR ¼ KILOGRAM VEGETABLES
5 candlenuts
3 small onions, minced
5 dried chillies
1 tsp shrimp paste, roasted
4 tbsps water
1 tbsp oil

### METHOD

1. Pound candlenuts, shrimp paste, onions and chillies to a coarse paste.
2. Heat oil, fry the paste until it no longer sticks to the pan.

# Thai Red Curry Paste for Meat/Vegetables
*(A Hot Blend)*

15 dried red chillies
 3 small onions, minced
 1 stalk lemon grass, chopped
10 black peppercorns
 4 cloves garlic, minced
 1 tbsp galangal powder
1½ tbsps coriander seeds
 1 tsp shrimp paste
 1 tsp lime rind, dried, soaked
 1 tsp caraway seeds
 1 tsp salt
 2 tbsps coriander roots, minced
 4 tbsp oil

### METHOD

1. Liquidise the coriander seeds, caraway seeds, peppercorns, chillies and galangal powder.
2. Pound the liquidised ingredients together with the other ingredients including oil to make a smooth paste.

### Note:
Store in an air tight jar in a refrigerator. It will keep for 1 month.

# Indian Curry Paste for Meat/ Vegetables
*(A Fairly Mild Blend)*

120 g coriander seeds
 15 g cumin seeds
 30 g peppercorns
 30 g turmeric
 30 g turmeric
  3 cloves garlic
 30 g dried chillies
 25 g mustard seeds
 15 g fresh ginger
 60 g lentils (yellow split)
Vinegar
Mustard oil

### METHOD

1.  Roast the spices. Combine with the other ingredients and grind or liquidise, blending in a little vinegar to make a thick paste.
2.  Fry in hot oil until browned. Keep in an air tight jar.

# Indo-Thai Curry Paste for Meat
*(A Mildly-hot Blend)*

FOR ¾ KILOGRAM MEAT
10 dried chillies
 4 cloves
 7 cloves garlic
 5 cardamom pods
 6 small onions, minced
 5 cm stick cinnamon
 2 bay leaves
1½ tsps lemon grass powder
1½ tsps galangal powder
 ½ tsp shrimp paste
 ½ tsp nutmeg powder
 ½ tsp salt

### METHOD

1.  Roast the cinnamon, cardamom pods, cloves, bay leaves, lemon grass and galangal powder lightly.
2.  Now put all the ingredients together and pound to a coarse fine paste.

### Note:
Add 1 litre of thick coconut milk.

# Indian Curry Paste for Meat
*(A Mild Blend)*

FOR 250 g MUTTON
½ tsp ginger paste
 1 tsp coriander powder
½ tsp garlic paste
 1 tbsp oil
½ tsp chilli powder
 1 tsp turmeric powder
 1 onion, sliced, fried and ground

### METHOD

1.  Mix all the freshly ground and powdered ingredients and fry them in oil with the meat.

### Note:
Add ¼ litre of water or lentil water boiled with 5 tablespoons of yellow split lentils.

# Indonesian Curry Paste for Seafood
*(A Fairly Hot Blend)*

FOR 1 KILOGRAM FISH
10 dried chillies
10 small onions
 3 red chillies
 5 candlenuts
 4 cloves garlic
 1 tbsp oil
 2 tbsps coriander seeds
 1 tsp shrimp paste
 1 tsp lemon grass
 2 slices galangal
 1 cm piece turmeric

### METHOD

1.  Grind or liquidise all the ingredients to a smooth paste.
2.  Heat one tablespoon oil, saute ground ingredients until fragrant.

### Note:
1 litre coconut milk is added.

# Jaffna Curry Paste for Prawns
*(A Fairly Hot Blend)*

FOR ½ KILOGRAM PRAWNS
10 dried chillies
80 g grated coconut
4 cloves garlic
2 cm piece fresh turmeric
40 ml coconut milk
½ tsp fenugreek seeds
1 tsp garam masala
1 tbsp coriander seeds
2 cm piece fresh ginger
7 curry leaves

### METHOD
1. Grind or liquidise the above ingredients to a smooth paste.
2. Add coconut milk to make a smooth paste. Add to partially fried prawns and cook.

# Indian Korma Curry Paste for Fish
*(A Mild Blend)*

FOR ½ KILOGRAM FISH
45 g coriander seeds
30 g garlic
6 dried chillies
7 cloves
250 ml curd
1 tsp black peppercorns
1 tsp cumin seeds, fried
2 cardamom pods
4 cm stick cinnamon
Salt to taste

### METHOD
1. Grind or liquidise all the spices and combine it with the curd.
2. Add salt to taste. Use as required.

# Thai Orange Curry Paste for Sour Shrimp Soups

2 small onions
½ tbsp shrimp paste
½ tsp vinegar
6 dried chillies, soaked
½ tsp salt

### METHOD
1. Pound onions, chillies, shrimp paste, salt, adding vinegar until the paste is smooth. Use as required.

# Malay Curry Paste for Fish
*(A Sour Blend)*

FOR ½ KILOGRAM OF FISH
10 dried chillies
3 small onions, minced
3 cloves garlic
2 stalks lemon grass
1 tsp shrimp paste, roasted
1 tsp galangal powder
½ tsp turmeric powder
1 tbsp tamarind concentrate
1 tbsp oil

### METHOD
1. Grind or liquidise all the ingredients into a smooth paste.
2. Dilute tamarind concentrate in 100 ml water.
3. Heat the paste in oil until lightly brown. Add tamarind water.

# Sauces,
# Dressings & Dips

*"Epicurean cooks
Sharpen with cloyness
sauce his appetite.*

— William Shakespeare

# English Creamy Curry Sauce for Lobsters/Prawns

 60 g butter
250 ml milk
Pinch of pepper
 2 tsps curry powder for seafood
 1 tbsp flour
Salt to taste

### METHOD

1. Stir in the curry powder in the heated butter and cook over a low heat stirring two to three times.
2. Add flour, pepper and salt and mix until well blended.
3. Simmer for a moment until the mixture is thick and smooth.
4. Add in the milk and prawns or lobsters.

Note:
This sauce may also be used for fish or vegetables.

# Indonesian Hot Sauce for Braised Fish

125 ml thick coconut milk
2½ tsps lemon juice
3½ tbsps Javanese soya sauce
 1 tsp chilli powder
 ½ tsp salt

### METHOD

1. Combine all the ingredients and allow to simmer for 5 – 7 minutes. Pour sauce over braised fish.

# Indian Tomato Sauce for Prawns

 3 large tomatoes
 5 cloves garlic, ground
250 ml water
 60 g brown sugar
2½ tsps chilli powder
1½ tsps vinegar

### METHOD

1. Boil, skin and mash the tomatoes.
2. Add garlic, sugar and chilli powder and continue to simmer until the liquid comes to a boil.
3. Add vinegar. Stir for a minute, remove.

# English Curry Sauce for Fish

 60 g butter
 60 g flour
500 ml milk
 2 tbsps curry powder
 2 tbsps vinegar
 2 tsps sugar
Salt/pepper to taste

### METHOD

1. Combine curry powder, sugar and vinegar.
2. Melt butter, fry flour until it changes colour.
3. Gradually add milk, stirring continuously so that lumps will not be formed.
4. Add combined ingredients and mix well before removing from the fire. Cook for a minute. Add pepper and salt.

Note:
This sauce can be mixed with fish, or boiled eggs or served on lettuce.

# English Yogurt Sauce for Cooked Cabbage/Cauliflower

225 ml yogurt
 1 small onion, minced
Pinch of pepper
 1 tsp curry powder
 2 tbsps butter
Salt to taste

### METHOD

1. Saute onion lightly in heated butter and then remove.
2. Add curry powder and fry until it changes colour.
3. Then add onion, pepper, salt and yogurt. Simmer until a smooth sauce is formed. This sauce can be used like mayonnaise.

# Chinese Sauce for Barbecued Pork

7 tbsps dark sweet soya sauce
2 red chillies, pounded
½ tsp tamarind juice
½ tsp sesame oil

---

METHOD

1. Combine all the ingredients and serve with barbecued pork.

# Singaporean Sauce for Rice Noodles

150 g small onions, chopped
450 ml coconut milk
  2 cloves garlic, chopped
  2 slices ginger, chopped
  4 cashew nuts, blanched
  1 tbsp shrimp paste
  1 tbsp candlenut powder
½ tsp turmeric powder
  3 tbsps peanut oil
Salt to taste

---

METHOD

1. Pound garlic, onions, ginger, nuts and shrimp paste.
2. Combine with turmeric powder, salt and candlenut powder.
3. Heat oil, fry the pounded ingredients for 3 minutes.
4. Add coconut milk and simmer for 10 minutes.

# Straits Chinese Sauce for Noodles

400 ml coconut milk
  2 small onions, chopped
  2 cloves garlic, chopped
  6 red chillies, sliced, ground
  1 tsp coriander seeds, ground
½ tsp chilli powder
½ tsp sesame oil
½ tsp turmeric powder
  3 tbsps peanut oil
  1 tsp ginger, ground
Salt to taste

---

METHOD

1. Blend oils and saute onion, garlic and ginger.
2. Add the spices, stirring for a minute or two.
3. Gradually add the coconut milk and season with salt.

# Singaporean Fried Bean Curd Sauce

112 g peanuts, roasted, pounded
 30 g dried prawns, pounded
  4 red chillies, pounded
  3 green chillies, pounded
2½ tsps thick soya sauce
  1 tbsp vinegar
  1 tbsp sugar
200 ml warm water
Salt to taste

---

METHOD

1. Combine all the ingredients until the sauce is of a smooth consistency.
2. Add salt to taste. Pour over fried soya bean curd cakes.

# Indian Curd Sauce for Plain Cooked Rice
*(A Mild Blend)*

750 ml curd
  2 green chillies, minced
  1 small onion, sliced
  1 red/dried chilli, sliced
 10 curry leaves
 20 g coconut
  1 sprig curry leaves, sauted
¼ tsp mustard seeds
  1 tsp yellow split lentils
  1 tsp rice
¼ tsp turmeric powder
¼ tsp minced ginger
  2 tsps ghee
Salt to taste

---

METHOD

1. Soak rice and lentils together in 250 ml water for 2 hours.
2. Liquidise or grind the soaked ingredients, green chillies, ginger, coconut, onion and curry leaves into a smooth paste.
3. Combine the curd with turmeric powder and salt. Churn the curd till smooth. Then add the paste.
4. Heat ghee, add the sprig of curry leaves, red chilli, and mustard seeds and when mustard seeds begin to splutter, add the curd mixture. Remove when it bubbles through.

# Indonesian Peanut Sauce for Skewered Meat

120 g fried peanuts, ground
350 ml water
100 ml coconut milk
  2 cloves, ground
  2 small onions, ground
  6 red chillies, ground
Oil for frying
  1 tbsp Javanese soya sauce
  1 tbsp brown sugar
  1 tbsp oil
  1 tsp shrimp paste, roasted
½ tsp ginger, ground
  1 tsp salt
  1 tbsp lemon juice

---

METHOD

1.  Combine the ground ingredients (except peanuts) and pound together with shrimp paste.
2.  Heat two tablespoons oil, fry the combined ingredients, stirring continuously. Add water. When it begins to boil add soya sauce, peanuts, sugar, lemon juice, coconut milk and salt. Continue to stir until the sauce thickens.

    Note:
    Use as a dip for skewered meat, as a meat sauce, or with eggs and cold vegetables.

# Thai Peanut Sauce for Skewered Meat

7½ tbsps peanut butter
275 ml thick coconut milk
  1 stalk lemon grass, sliced
  1 small onion, minced
  1 tbsp fish sauce
  1 tbsp palm sugar
  1 tbsp sweet soya sauce (dark)
1¼ tsps chilli powder (cayenne)

---

METHOD

1.  Combine all the ingredients and bring to a boil, stirring well. Use as a dip for skewered meat or serve as a sauce with meat.

# Malay Sauce for Skewered Meat

112 g roasted peanuts
250 ml coconut milk, thick
  2 small onions, minced
  2 cloves garlic, minced
  5 tbsps tamarind water
  4 red chillies, ground
juice of a small lemon
  2 tsps coriander seeds
  1 tsp fennel seeds
  1 tsp cumin seeds
  1 tsp brown sugar
  3 tbsps peanut oil
  1 tsp shrimp paste
Salt to taste

---

METHOD

1.  Liquidise or grind all the dry spices. Pound peanuts coarsely.
2.  Heat oil, fry shrimp paste, onion, garlic and ground chilli for two minutes. Add peanuts, sugar, ground spices, tamarind water, coconut milk and salt.
3.  Continue to simmer until a smooth sauce is formed. Stir in the lemon juice before serving.

# Pacific Island Coconut Sauce
*(A Mild Blend)*

500 ml coconut milk
  1 small onion, sliced
  1 clove garlic, sliced
  4 cm piece ginger root, chopped
  1 tbsp curry powder
3½ tbsps olive oil
  4 tbsps flour
Salt to taste

---

METHOD

1.  Blend curry powder and flour.
2.  Saute onion lightly and then add blended ingredients and fry until dark brown.
3.  Stir in the coconut milk, onion, garlic, ginger root and salt.
4.  Simmer until the sauce is smooth. Remove ginger root and serve with meat dishes or vegetables.

Note:
Add to cooked vegetables or meat before removing from the fire.

# Indian Coconut Sauce
*(A Mild Blend)*

¼ medium sized coconut
1 green chilli, sliced
3 cloves garlic, sliced
2 small onions, sliced
250 ml water
1 tsp oil
½ tsp vegetable curry powder
½ tsp peppercorns, fried
½ tsp cumin seeds, fried
1 tsp tamarind water
¼ tsp turmeric powder
¼ tsp mustard seeds
Salt to taste

METHOD

1. Grind or liquidise the coconut, chilli, garlic, onions, cumin seeds, peppercorns, salt, and blend with the water.
2. Heat oil, fry mustard seeds and when it starts to splutter, add the blended ingredients together with turmeric powder, curry powder, tamarind water.
3. Bring to a boil. Remove from heat.

Note:
Add cooked lentils or green vegetables.

# Singaporean Fruit and Vegetable Salad Sauce

13 dried chillies, ground
20 small onions, ground
112 g peanuts, roasted, pounded fine
550 ml tamarind water
112 g mashed sweet potato
2 tsps shrimp paste, roasted
3½ tbsps oil
Sugar and salt to taste

METHOD

1. Pound the ground ingredients and shrimp paste together.
2. Heat oil, fry the pounded ingredients until cooked.
3. Add peanuts, a little tamarind water and gradually add the mashed sweet potato, the remaining tamarind water, sugar and salt.
4. Boil on a slow fire until it is well cooked.

# Indonesian Sauce for Boiled Vegetables

125 g roasted peanuts, ground
250 ml water
275 ml coconut milk
3 cloves garlic, minced
4 small onions, minced
1 tbsp tamarind concentrate
4 red chillies
2 slices galangal
1 tsp shrimp paste
½ tsp brown sugar
½ tsp chilli powder
Peanut oil
3 candlenuts
Salt to taste

METHOD

1. Pound shrimp paste, garlic, onions, candlenut, galangal, red chillies and salt.
2. Dilute tamarind concentrate with the water.
3. Heat 3 tbsps oil and fry the pounded ingredients until fragrant.
4. Add sugar and chilli powder. Stir well.
5. Add tamarind water with coconut milk.
6. Stir well and when it begins to bubble, add peanuts. Allow to simmer until it begins to thicken. Remove.

Note:
Pour this sauce over boiled potatoes, bean sprouts, string beans, partially boiled shredded vegetables and slices of boiled eggs.

# Straits Chinese Sauce for Vegetables

150 g roasted peanuts
112 g tamarind pulp
2 tsps shrimp paste, fried, pounded
250 ml water
1 tbsp chilli paste
2 tbsps sugar
½ tbsp salt

METHOD

1. Dilute tamarind pulp in water and strain.
2. Pound peanuts coarsely. Combine with the chilli paste, shrimp paste, salt and sugar in a large bowl.
3. Combine with tamarind water and peanuts. Add more water according to desired consistency

22

# Spicy Sweet Sauce for Fruit and Vegetable Salad

2 tbsps chilli paste
4 tbsps lemon juice
3 tbsps oil
4 tbsps Javanese soya sauce
8 tbsps brown sugar
1 tsp shrimp paste
200 ml thick coconut milk
Salt to taste

## METHOD

1. Pound chilli paste, sugar, shrimp paste, lemon juice and salt.
2. Saute the pounded ingredients in oil until it gives out an aroma.
3. Add coconut milk and soya sauce. Cool. Serve over fruit and vegetable salad.

# Thai Hot Sauce for Raw Vegetables Salad

13 g dried prawns, pounded
4 cloves garlic
9 dried chillies
Juice of a lime fruit
1 tbsp sugar
1 tbsp fish sauce
2 tsps shrimp paste
Salt to taste

## METHOD

1. Liquidise or grind the chillies and then add the garlic, prawns, sugar, salt, fish sauce and shrimp paste.
2. Remove when it combines to a thick sauce. Add lime juice. Serve over raw vegetables.

# Thai Hot Sauce for Boiled Vegetables

10 dried red chillies, soaked
6 cloves garlic, chopped
2 small onions, chopped
1 large onion, chopped
4 tsps shrimp paste
Salt to taste

## METHOD

1. Roast the shrimp paste in foil.
2. Combine all the ingredients and liquidise or grind with a little water. Add salt.

## Note:

Pour this sauce over boiled radish, watercress, cabbage, cucumber and carrot strips. Or serve it in a bowl with the boiled vegetables.

# Thai Dressing for Salad

4 cloves garlic, chopped
4 red chillies, sliced
1 tbsp fish sauce
1½ tbsps lemon juice
2 tsps sugar

## METHOD

Pound garlic and chillies and then add fish sauce, lemon juice, sugar and mix well.
Pour this dressing over salad.

# Indian Coconut Dressing for Salads

80 ml thick coconut milk
20 ml lemon juice
1 tbsp coriander leaves, chopped
½ tsp chilli powder
1 small onion, minced
Salt to taste

## METHOD

Combine all the ingredients and serve on salads.

*Curry Sauces and Dressings.*

# Indian Yogurt Dressing for Salads

80 ml yogurt
Juice of a small lemon
1 tbsp coriander leaves, chopped
1 green chilli, minced
2 small onions, minced
Salt to taste

METHOD

Combine all the ingredients and serve on salads.

# Indian Almond Dressing for Raw Salads

60 g almond, ground
60 ml yogurt
60 ml lemon juice
2 tsps honey
½ tsp chilli powder
Salt to taste

METHOD

Combine all the ingredients and serve on salads.

# Jaffna Dip for Boiled Tapioca

10 red chillies
1 tsp tamarind water
Salt to taste

METHOD

Pound the chillies, salt and add tamarind water.

# Cambodian/Vietnamese Dressing for Salads

1 tsp coriander seeds, ground
1 tsp black peppercorns, ground
4½ tbsps lemon juice
1 tsp pounded garlic
½ tsp chilli powder
1½ tsps sugar
1 tsp salt

METHOD

Combine all the ingredients and serve.

# Indonesian Dressing for Salads

175 g roasted peanuts, pounded
55 g sugar
50 ml vinegar
1 red chilli, pounded
4 cloves garlic, pounded
Salt to taste

METHOD

Combine all the ingredients together and serve with salads.

# Indonesian Ginger Dip

1 tsp red chilli paste
½ tsp sugar
1 tsp cornstarch
125 ml water
1 tsp ginger, ground
2½ tsps dark sweet soya sauce
¼ tsp salt

METHOD

Combine in a saucepan all the ingredients and simmer slowly until it thickens.
Use as a dip for fish or serve over fried fish.

# Indonesian Dip for Barbecued Meat

350 g roasted peanuts, ground
6 cloves garlic, ground
13 dried chillies, ground
250 ml coconut milk, thick
5 candlenuts, ground
7 small onions, sliced
Salt, sugar and tamarind water to taste

METHOD

Heat oil, fry onions to golden colour. Then add the other ingredients. Bring to a boil and simmer it into a thick sauce.
Use as a dip for barbecued meat.

# Marinades

*"Appetite comes with eating."*

*— Old saying*

# Chinese Soya Sauce Marinade for Barbecued Spare Ribs

FOR 1 KILOGRAM SPARE RIBS
  2 cloves garlic, crushed
  1 tbsp crushed ginger
  1 tbsp sugar
  3 tbsps light soya sauce
  1 tbsp dry sherry
1½ tsps five-spice mixture
  ½ tsp salt

## METHOD

1. Combine garlic, ginger, sugar, soya sauce, sherry, five-spice mixture and rub meat with this mixture and then salt. Leave for 12 hours, turning and basting often.
2. Put in a greased roasting pan or on a rack in a shallow roasting pan. Roast in a 175°C oven, basting with the marinade frequently.
3. Cut into individual ribs.

Note:
The ribs may be cut before marinating, for greater crispness.

# Straits Chinese Coconut Milk Marinade for Barbecued Pork

FOR ½ KILOGRAM PORK
  7 red chillies
  7 candlenuts
  2 large onions, sliced
  2 stalks lemon grass, sliced thinly
125 ml coconut milk
  2 tsps sugar
  1 tsp shrimp paste
2½ tsps coriander seeds
  3 tbsps oil
Salt to taste

## METHOD

1. Cut pork into 2 cm cubes.
2. Pound the chillies, candlenuts, onions, shrimp paste, coriander seeds, sugar and salt.
3. Combine with oil and coconut milk. Marinate the meat and add in the lemon grass. Leave it for 2 hours. Barbecue or grill.

# French Wine Marinade for Roasted Pork Chops

FOR 4 PORK CHOPS
250 ml dry white wine
  1 bay leaf
  ½ tsp pepper
Drippings/fat for roasting
  7 peppercorns, whole
  1 small onion, whole
  1 clove, whole
Salt to taste

## METHOD

1. Combine bay leaf, onion, peppercorn, pepper, clove and wine.
2. Sprinkle salt over the pork chops and pour the marinade and leave to stand for 12 hours.
3. Remove chops from marinade and dry.
4. Heat fat in a roasting pan and roast the chops in a pre-heated oven, basting with the fat for 15 minutes. Then add the marinade, cooking and basting until the meat is tender.

# Thai/Burmese Fish Sauce Marinade For Pork Chops

FOR ½ KILOGRAM PORK CHOPS
  4 cloves garlic, chopped
  15 g coriander roots
  8 peppercorns
  1 tbsp fish sauce
1½ tbsps light soya sauce
  1 tbsp oil

## METHOD

1. Pound garlic, coriander roots, peppercorns, and combine with the fish sauce, soya sauce and oil.
2. Rub the chops with mixture and marinate for 1 hour. Roast or grill.

# Indian Onion Marinade for Fried Veal/Mutton

FOR ½ KILOGRAM VEAL OR MUTTON
250 g onion paste
1 tsp garlic paste
1¼ tsps garam masala
¼ tsp chilli paste
1 tsp ginger paste
¼ tsp turmeric paste
1 tsp salt
Ghee for frying

### METHOD

1. Debone and chop the meat into small pieces.
2. Combine onion, garlic, garam masala, ginger, turmeric, chilli and salt.
3. Rub this mixture into the meat and let it stand for 1½ hours.
4. Heat ghee, add meat mixture and fry until quite dry over a slow fire.

# Iranian Arrack Marinade for Skewered Lamb

FOR ½ KILOGRAM LAMB, CUBED
5 peppercorns, crushed
1 clove garlic, minced
5 medium sized tomatoes, sliced
6 spring onions, minced
50 ml arrack
1¼ tbsps brown sugar
¼ tsp lime peel powder
3 tbsps olive oil
Salt to taste

### METHOD

1. Combine all the ingredients and marinate the lamb in this mixture for 12 hours, turning regularly.
2. Barbecue or grill.

# Afghanistan Curd Marinade for Barbecued Mutton

FOR ¼ KILOGRAM LEG MUTTON
250 ml curd
6 cloves garlic, crushed
1 tsp pepper
Pinch of turmeric
Salt to taste
13 small onions, cleaned, whole
7 small tomatoes, cubed
13 red/green chillies
½ lime fruit
Drippings/lard (melted)

### METHOD

1. Cut meat into cubes.
2. Combine curd with garlic, pepper, turmeric, lime juice and salt.
3. Combine mutton, 100 g drippings in curd mixture for 3 hours.
4. Then skewer a cube of meat, a small onion, a tomato cube, red chilli, green chilli and repeat until the skewer is filled. Brush with melted fat.
5. Barbecue or grill until meat is brown and tender.

# Indonesian Vinegar Marinade for Lamb Curry

FOR 1¼ KILOGRAMS LAMB, CUBED
250 ml cider vinegar
112 g small onions, minced
3 cloves garlic, minced
1 tsp ginger powder
6 tbsps peanut oil
2 tsps ground coriander
1 tsp ground cumin
1 tsp ground chilli
1 tsp shrimp paste, roasted
250 ml water

### METHOD

1. Marinate the 2 cm cubed lamb in the vinegar for 45 minutes.
2. Combine onion, garlic, ginger, coriander, cumin, chilli, shrimp paste and rub the marinated lamb in this mixture and allow to stand for another 30 minutes.
3. Heat oil, fry the marinated lamb until brown.
4. Stir in the water and cook over a low heat until meat is tender.

# Indonesian Sweet Marinade for Meat

FOR ½ KILOGRAM MEAT
10 small onions, pounded
 8 cloves garlic, pounded
 1 small lemon fruit juice
 4 tbsps oil
 4 tbsps water
 2 tbsps sugar
 2 tbsps soya sauce
 2 tbsps coriander seeds, ground coarsely

## METHOD

1. Cut the meat into thin strips. Mix oil and water.
2. Marinate the meat with sugar and leave for 45 minutes.
3. Then combine garlic, soya sauce, onions, coriander, and lemon juice with the marinated meat.
4. Skewer and grill over a charcoal fire, sprinkling with oil mixture and turning frequently until cooked.

# Malay-Indonesian Coconut Marinade for Broiled Meat

FOR 1¼ KILOGRAMS MEAT CHOPS
250 ml coconut milk
 12 small onions, minced
  2 cloves garlic, minced
  1 tsp chilli paste
 ¼ tsp turmeric powder
  1 tsp ginger powder
 ¼ tsp shrimp paste
  1 tsp salt

## METHOD

1. Combine onion, garlic, ginger, chilli, turmeric, shrimp paste and salt.
2. Pound them together to a paste and combine with the coconut milk.
3. Marinate the meat in this mixture for 3 – 4 hours, turning them regularly. Drain, reserving the marinade and cook over very low heat.
4. Heat the marinade and serve with the cooked meat.

# Chinese Spiced Soya Sauce Marinade for Barbecued Chicken

FOR 1 KILOGRAM CHICKEN, WHOLE
70 ml soya sauce
 2 cloves garlic, minced
½ tsp sugar
 1 tsp salt
¼ tsp pepper
 1 tsp five-spice mixture
 2 tbsps oil

## METHOD

1. Wash, dry the chicken.
2. Combine soya sauce, garlic, pepper, salt, sugar, five-spice mixture and oil.
3. Rub this mixture inside and on the chicken. Stand for 1 hour.
4. Place on a rack in a shallow roasting pan. Roast and baste the chicken frequently, turning until it is tender and brown.

# Indian Yogurt Marinade for Roasted Chicken

FOR MEDIUM SIZED CHICKEN
 30 g garlic
 20 g coriander seeds
 40 g lentils, fried
 15 g poppy seeds
  2 small onions, sliced
250 ml yogurt
  1 tbsp ghee
  5 cloves
  4 cardamom pods
  5 g cumin seeds
Chilli powder
Salt to taste

## METHOD

1. Fry the onion in ghee.
   Grind all the spices with garlic, onion, lentils, salt and chilli powder.
2. Combine above with yogurt.
3. Place the chicken in a deep bowl and pour the marinade over it and allow to stand for 3 – 4 hours.
4. Roast.

# Indonesian Peanut Marinade for Broiled Chicken/Duck

FOR 1 KILOGRAM CHICKEN
30 g ground peanut
30 g ground onion
 5 ground chilli
 1 tsp salt
65 ml lime juice

### METHOD

1. Cut the chicken into bite-sized pieces.
2. Combine the onion, chilli, peanut, lime juice and salt.
3. Rub the chicken pieces with this mixture and let it stand for 1½ hours, turning occasionally.
4. Thread the chicken pieces on skewers and arrange on oiled broiling pan and broil slowly, turning frequently until tender.
5. Serve with peanut sauce.

# Chinese Peppered Marinade for Steamed Fried Duck

FOR 1 KILOGRAM DUCKLING
 2 slices ginger root, minced
 2 small onions, minced
Oil
½ tbsp Szechuan peppercorn, ground
 1 tbsp salt

### METHOD

1. Combine the ginger root, onion, pepper and salt.
2. Rub duck thoroughly with this mixture.
3. Press hard on the breast bone to flatten duck. Chill overnight.
4. Then steam for 2 – 2½ hours and cool.
5. Heat oil, deep fry until brown and crisp. Serve whole.

# Pakistani Spiced Marinade for Fried Chicken

FOR MEDIUM SIZED CHICKEN
1 tsp chilli powder
1 tbsp garlic paste
2 tbsps fresh ground pepper
1 tbsp ginger paste
2 tbsps milk
Salt to taste

### METHOD

1. Combine all the ingredients and apply the mixture to the cleaned chicken.
2. Allow to stand for 45 minutes. Then fry.

# Indonesian Spiced Marinade for Grilled Chicken

FOR YOUNG CHICKEN
 6 red chillies, ground
 7 small onions, ground
125 ml tamarind water
 50 g melted butter
 1 tsp sugar
 ¼ tsp turmeric paste
 7 cloves garlic, ground
Salt to taste

### METHOD

1. Cut the chicken into 4 pieces and pound them a little to tenderize.
2. Combine all the ingredients and marinate the chicken for 1½ hours, turning occasionally.
3. Grill the chicken evenly on a charcoal stove adding melted butter.

# Pacific Islands Lemon Marinade for Shrimp

350 g shrimp, shelled, deveined
125 ml lemon juice
112 g onions, minced
 ¼ tsp black pepper, freshly ground
 ½ tsp salt

---

METHOD

1. Wash, dry and slice the shrimps in half, lengthwise.
2. Combine shrimps in a bowl with the lemon juice and onions. Marinate for at least 4 – 5 hours.
3. Season with salt and pepper.

Note:
The citrus flavour gives the shrimps a cooked flavour.

# Indian Egg Marinade for Fried Fish

 4 fish fillets
½ tsp ground chilli
 1 tbsp minced onion
1½ tbsps lemon juice
 2 eggs
 ¼ tsp turmeric powder
 1 clove garlic, pounded
Salt to taste
Oil for frying

---

METHOD

1. Combine the eggs, ground chilli, onion, garlic, turmeric powder, salt and lemon juice. Mix throughly and then put the fillets and marinate for 1 hour, turning occasionally.
2. Fry them until golden brown.

# Indian Spiced Marinade for Fried Fish

FOR ½ KILOGRAM FISH FILLETS
2 tsps coriander powder
½ tsp turmeric powder
1 tbsp fried and ground onion
1 tsp chilli powder
1 tsp garlic paste
½ tsp salt
Oil for frying

METHOD

1. Rub the spices over the fillets and leave them to marinate for 7 hours in a closed dish.
2. Then shallow fry.

# Indonesian Tamarind Marinade for Fish

FOR 1 KILOGRAM FISH FILLETS
125 ml tamarind juice
pinch of chilli powder
2 cloves garlic, crushed
Pinch of turmeric powder
Salt to taste

METHOD

1. Combine all the ingredients of the marinade and pour over the fish fillets.
2. Leave it for 30 minutes, turning the fish from time to time. Drain and fry or use as required.

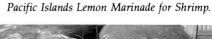

*Pacific Islands Lemon Marinade for Shrimp.*

# Caribbean Lime Marinade for Fried Fish

FOR ¼ KILOGRAM FISH FILLETS:
  1 large lime
  1 small onion, minced
  1 red chilli, minced
  1 spring onion, minced
½ tsp black pepper
  1 tbsp flour
  2 tsps salt
Oil for frying

### METHOD

1.  Wash the fish and rub with a teaspoon of salt and the juice of half a lime.
2.  Combine the other ingredients except the flour and oil for frying and allow the fish fillets to marinate for an hour.
3.  Then dip in flour and fry in heated oil.

# Chinese Soya Sauce Marinade for Grilled Prawns

10 king-sized prawns, shelled, deveined, tails intact
  2 tbsps light soya sauce
  1 tsp ginger juice
  1 tbsp dry sherry
¼ tsp salt
½ tbsp sugar
Oil

### METHOD

1.  Combine light soya sauce, ginger juice, dry sherry, salt, sugar and prawns. Marinate for 1½ hours.
2.  Thread on skewers, brush with peanut oil and grill. Brush with more oil as the prawns cook.

# Garnishes

*"Garnishes and decorations add texture, colour, appeal and contrast to a dish."*

# Garnishes for
## Indian Steamed Fish Curry
## Indian Fish Head Curry

FOR 450 g FISH
1 large onion
4 cm piece fresh ginger
4 cloves garlic
2 green chillies
2 red chillies

---

METHOD

1. Slice onions into rings and fry till crisp and brown.
2. Slice ginger and garlic into long, fine strips.
3. Slice chillies.
4. Put curry into a large platter and garnish.

# Garnishes for
## Indian Lamb Chops
## New Zealand Lamb Chops
## Indonesian Lamb Chops

FOR 450 g MEAT
1 large onion
2 tomatoes
2 sprigs coriander leaves
2 green chillies
1 small cucumber
1 small lemon

---

METHOD

1. Chop tomatoes, cucumber and chillies.
2. Slice onion thinly.
3. Slice half of lemon thinly.
4. Garnish with ingredients and squeeze in juice of remaining lemon.

# Garnishes for
## Burmese Pork Meatballs
## Indian Curried Meatballs

FOR 450 g MEAT
1 large onion, sliced thinly
1 small lemon, sliced thinly
2 sprigs mint or coriander leaves
3 red chillies, sliced
3 green chillies, sliced

# Garnishes for
## Indonesian Chicken Broth
## Thai Corn and Prawn Soup

FOR 2 LITRES SOUP
Onion flakes, sauteed
1 red chilli, thinly sliced
Coriander leaves, chopped
2 spring onions, chopped

---

METHOD

1. Sprinkle garnish into soup just before serving.

# Garnishes for
## Curried Eggs

FOR 6 EGGS
1 red chilli, deseeded, thinly sliced
1 green chilli, deseeded, thinly sliced
Parsley, chopped
1 small lemon, wedged
3 gherkins

# Garnishes for
## Indian Fish Biriani
## Indian Chicken Biriani
## Indian Mutton Biriani
## Armenian Lamb Biriani

FOR 450 g RICE
15 almonds, blanched
1 tbsp raisins
Edible silver foil
1 large onion
2 hard boiled eggs, shelled
Oil

---

METHOD

1. Slice onions thinly and fry till crisp.
2. Brown almonds and raisins in oil.
3. Slice boiled eggs thickly.
4. Place rice on a platter and decorate with ingredients topped with silver foil.

Note:
Edible silver foil or Varak is said to aid digestion and is available at Indian food suppliers.

# Garnishes for
## Basic Soup
## Curry Soup
## British Mulligatawny

FOR 2 LITRES SOUP
Parsley, chopped
Toasted almonds, chopped
Cooked vegetables, thinly sliced

# Garnishes for
## Meat Curries

FOR 450 g MEAT
4 small potatoes, roasted
2 sprigs mint or coriander leaves
Cooked green peas
2 red chillies, thinly sliced

METHOD

1. Cook ingredients in boiling salted water.
2. Garnish just before serving.

*Garnishes for Lamb Chops.*

# Garnishes for
## Ghee Rice
## Prawn Biriani

FOR 450 g RICE
1 large onion
1 sprig curry leaves
1 tsp mustard seeds
2 red chillies
Oil

METHOD

1. Slice onion thinly and fry till crisp.
2. Cut chillies into strips and saute with the curry leaves.
3. Add mustard seeds and when they begin to splutter remove.
4. Place rice in a serv ng platter and garnish with ingredients.

# Garnishes for
## Indonesian Fish Stew
## Indonesian Fish Curry

FOR 450 g FISH
3 large red chillies
1 small lemon

METHOD

1. Cut chillies into strips.
2. Slice lemon thinly.
3. Arrange fish curry on platter, pour sauce over and garnish.

# Rice & Noodles

*We lack but open eye and ear*
*To find the Orient's marvels here.*
*(John Whittier, The Chapel of the Hermits)*

# Sri Lankan Ghee Rice

455 g Patna rice
125 g ghee
1 litre vegetable stock
1 sprig curry leaves
50 g cashew nuts, roasted
1 tbsp curry powder for vegetable
60 g raisins, fried
15 peppercorns, freshly ground
45 g small onions, sliced
3 cardamom pods
4 cloves
5 cm stick cinnamon
Salt to taste

---

METHOD

1. Heat ghee, fry onions, curry leaves, curry powder, cardamom pods, cloves, cinnamon, pepper, salt for 3 – 4 minutes over a medium heat.
2. Gradually add rice stirring for another 3 minutes.
3. Add stock, cover and simmer on a low heat until rice is dry and fluffy.
4. Add cashew nuts and raisins, mix thoroughly with the rice before removing it from the pan.

Note:
For garnish see page 36.

# Indian Kedgeree

115 g dhall/lentils
225 g Patna rice
1 litre water
60 g ghee
1 large onion, minced
1 clove garlic, crushed
1 tsp turmeric powder
¼ tsp ground cloves
½ tsp ground cinnamon
1 tsp cardamom powder
Salt and pepper to taste

---

METHOD

1. Saute the onion and garlic in heated ghee until tender.
2. Stir in the spices and salt, fry for a minute or two.
3. Add water and bring to the boil then add in the lentils and rice.
4. Cover and simmer for approximately 35 – 45 minutes so that all moisture is absorbed and the rice is cooked.

# Hindu Temple Rice

300 g cooked rice
350 ml yogurt/curd
1 tsp mustard seeds
1 tbsp vegetable oil
1 tbsp unsalted butter/ghee
3 red chillies, minced
1 tsp minced ginger
Salt to taste

---

METHOD

1. Before the rice cools, add unsalted butter or ghee.
2. Mix well, then add curd or yogurt, red chillies, ginger, salt and stir thoroughly.
3. In a small saucepan, fry the mustard seeds in oil till it crackles, then pour it over the rice mixture, stir and serve.

# Sri Lanka Milk Rice, Sinhalese Style

450 g raw rice
400 ml coconut milk, thin
500 ml coconut milk, thick
Salt to taste

METHOD

1.  Add the second extraction of coconut milk with rice and bring to a boil.
2.  When the rice has absorbed all the liquid, add salt and the thick coconut milk, stir, lower the heat and allow to simmer until the rice is dry and cooked.

# Sri Lanka Milk Rice (Jaffna Style)

450 g uncooked rice
225 g green grams, roasted, split
Salt to taste
800 ml fresh cow's milk
300 ml water

METHOD

1.  Bring the water to a boil on a high heat.
2.  Add rice and green grams and cook until all the water has nearly been absorbed.
3.  Add milk and salt. Mix thoroughly, then cover and simmer until rice is cooked.

*Hindu Temple Rice.*

# Indonesian Fried Rice

455 g cooked rice
120 g pork, diced
50 g shrimp, shelled
3 cloves garlic, chopped
1 small onion, chopped
1 large onion
7 red chillies, chopped
¼ bunch spring onions, chopped
Peanut oil
3 eggs
½ tsp turmeric powder
2 tsps chilli powder
1 tsp ground ginger
1 tsp shrimp paste
1 tbsp Javanese soya sauce
4 tbsps tamarind water
¼ tsp pepper powder
1 tbsp milk
1 small cucumber, skinned, sliced thinly
Salt to taste

### METHOD

1. Pound onion, garlic, ginger, shrimp paste, pepper, turmeric, chilli powder finely.
2. Saute the mixture in two tablespoons of oil, adding soya sauce, tamarind water, salt, red chillies, shrimp and pork.
3. Stir well to combine all the ingredients including rice over low heat.
4. Lightly beat the eggs with milk, some pepper and salt and fry this mixture into an omelette.
5. Slice large onion and fry till brown and crisp.
6. Serve the rice with spring onions, cucumber, fried onions and omelette cut into thin strips.

# Indonesian Coconut Rice

455 g long grain rice
1 litre coconut milk, thick or thin
2 cm lemon grass, bruised
Salt to taste

### METHOD

1. Combine coconut milk, lemon grass, salt and bring to the boil with a tight fitting lid.
2. Add rice and cook over a low heat until all the liquid has evaporated.

# Indonesian Chicken Rice

455 g long grain Patna rice
455 g chicken, disjointed
980 ml coconut milk
5 small onions, crushed
4 candlenuts, ground
½ tsp lemon grass powder
¼ tsp galangal powder
¼ tsp turmeric powder
2 tsps coriander powder
1 tsp shrimp paste
3 laurel leaves (daun salam)
Salt to taste

### METHOD

1. Cook chicken pieces in 500 ml coconut milk with onions, shrimp paste, lemon grass powder, galangal powder, candlenut paste, coriander, cumin powders and salt.
2. Boil rice with 480 ml coconut milk until nearly cooked.
3. Remove the chicken pieces from the gravy and add in the rice.
4. Boil the rice in the gravy for sometime, then put in the chicken pieces.
5. Steam until the flavour of the chicken is well spread throughout the rice.
6. Add laurel leaves, before removing pot from the fire.

# Indonesian Spiced Rice

235 g long grain rice
500 ml coconut milk
40 g peanuts, roasted
1 tsp shrimp paste
1 tsp cumin powder
1 tsp lemon grass powder
2 small onions, sliced
2 cloves garlic, crushed
4 dried red chillies, soaked
1½ tsps coriander powder
4 tbsps peanut oil
½ tsp turmeric powder
Salt to taste

### METHOD

1. Boil the rice in coconut milk until rice is dry and fluffy.
2. Pound onions, garlic, chillies, shrimp paste, coriander powder, cumin powder, lemon grass powder, peanuts, turmeric powder and salt.
3. Fry the pounded ingredients in heated oil until an aroma is given out.
4. Now add the rice and mix thoroughly.

# Thai Fried Rice

450 g cooked rice
150 g prawns cooked, shelled
125 g pork cooked, diced
  1 small cucumber, peeled, sliced
  5 spring onions, chopped
  1 lime, cut into wedges
  2 eggs, well-beaten
1½ tbsps fish sauce
2½ tbsps tomato ketchup
  1 large onion, minced
  3 cloves garlic, minced
  3 tbsps vegetable oil
Coriander leaves
Pinch of salt/pepper

---

METHOD

1. Heat oil, brown garlic and onion lightly.
2. Add prawns, pork and fish sauce and stir for a couple of minutes.
3. Add rice, stirring well; then add pepper, salt and tomato ketchup.
4. Gradually add in the eggs, stirring until well mixed and set.
5. Transfer to a dish; garnish with spring onions, coriander leaves, cucumber slices and lime wedges.

# Malay Yellow Rice

455 g long grain rice
250 g small onions, sliced, pounded
100 g dried prawns, soaked, pounded
  1 litre coconut milk
  1 tsp ground turmeric powder
  2 tsps minced garlic, pounded
  5 cm lemon grass, chopped, pounded
 12 peppercorns, crushed
  6 cloves
  5 tbsps peanut oil
  1 tsp cardamom powder
Salt to taste

---

METHOD

1. Fry pounded ingredients: prawns, lemon grass, garlic and onions for a minute or two.
2. Add washed, drained rice and stir continuously for 3 – 4 minutes.
3. Turn the heat up to medium from low. Add coconut milk, salt, crushed peppercorns, cloves, turmeric powder and cardamom powder. Cover, allow to simmer until the rice is dry and fluffy.

# Indian Yellow Rice

225 g long grain rice
100 g ghee
  2 cloves garlic, crushed
  2 small onions, minced
450 ml water
  1 sprig curry leaves
  3 cloves
  2 cardamom pods
2.5 cm stick cinnamon
  1 tsp cumin, ground
 ½ tsp turmeric powder
Salt to taste

---

METHOD

1. Wash and soak rice for half hour, then drain thoroughly.
2. Blend turmeric powder and cumin with a tablespoon water.
3. Saute onions, curry leaves, garlic, cinnamon, cardamom pods, cloves in moderately heated ghee until onions become soft.
4. Add blended ingredients and water; stir for a while, then add the rice seasoned with salt.
5. Allow to cook on a high heat for 5 minutes, then lower the heat, cover and cook the rice until dry and fluffy.

# Chinese Fried Rice

455 g cooked rice
125 g barbecued pork, cubed
225 g cooked, peeled prawns
  3 eggs, well-beaten
  4 tbsps sesame oil
  1 clove garlic, crushed
  2 spring onions, chopped
  4 tbsps water
  2 tbsps light soya sauce
  1 tsp monosodium glutamate
Pepper and salt to taste

---

METHOD

1. Heat one teaspoon oil and scramble the eggs. Remove.
2. Heat some more oil and fry the garlic, prawns, pork and adding a dash of soya sauce. Remove.
3. Now fry the rice with soya sauce mixed with water, one teaspoon salt, and monosodium glutamate.
4. Stir well, adding all the other ingredients. Stir fry till rice is thoroughly coated with sauce mixture.

# Burmese Chicken Noodles

455 g vermicelli, cooked, drained
500 ml coconut milk
 70 ml oil
455 g chicken
 25 small onions, chopped
  4 cloves garlic, crushed
250 ml water
 ½ tsp chilli powder
  1 tsp turmeric powder
  1 tsp shrimp paste
  1 tsp fish sauce
  2 tsps ginger, minced
1½ tbsps flour
Pepper and salt to taste

### METHOD

1. Wash, dry and rub chicken with turmeric powder and salt.
2. Boil chicken in boiling water until chicken is cooked, then bone and cut into bite size pieces.
3. Reduce the chicken gravy by half its stock, then remove.
4. Fry onions, garlic, ginger and shrimp paste into a paste. Remove and pound.
5. Heat oil again, fry the pounded ingredients for a minute or two over a medium heat.
6. Add chicken to the paste, fry until brown.
7. Add stock and gradually, the flour mixed with coconut milk, fish sauce, chilli powder, pepper and salt.
8. Cook over a medium heat for a minute, then lower the heat until the gravy has thickened, then add the noodles. Mix thoroughly and remove.

# Indian Fried Noodles

300 g yellow fresh noodles
 50 g bean sprouts, cleaned
  1 medium sized potato, cooked, diced
  2 eggs
  1 small onion, chopped
  2 firm bean curd cakes, diced
 30 spring greens, cut into 2.5 cm pieces
Oil
 70 g minced mutton, cooked
  2 small tomatoes, chopped, diced
  3 green chillies, sliced
  1 tbsp tomato ketchup
  1 tbsp chilli sauce
  2 tsp soya sauce
  2 red chillies, sliced
Salt to taste

### METHOD

1. Heat 7 tablespoons oil, fry bean curd pieces until brown. Remove.
2. Add more oil, and fry onion, noodles, tomato pieces, sauces, tomato ketchup and salt for 4 minutes.
3. Then add spring greens, bean sprouts and continue to fry for a few more minutes.
4. Add eggs, scramble and when nearly set, add potato, fried bean curd pieces, chillies, mutton. Add more sauce if required.
5. Serve with sliced cucumber, tomato sauce and a wedge of lime.

# Indonesian Noodles with Vegetables

455 g egg noodles, cooked, drained
255 g bean sprouts, cleaned
100 g cauliflower, chopped
100 g cabbage, shredded
125 g prawns, shelled, halved
  3 eggs
Peanut oil
  2 tsps black pepper, freshly ground
  1 tsp Javanese soya sauce
  1 tsp minced fresh ginger
 ½ tsp. shrimp paste
  5 small onions, sliced
  3 cloves garlic, minced
Salt to taste

### METHOD

1. Fry onions, garlic in two tablespoons oil until onions change colour.
2. Add more oil then add shrimp paste, ginger, pepper, prawns, vegetables, bean sprouts, soya sauce, salt and gradually stir in the eggs until well mixed.
3. Add drained noodles and let the whole thing simmer until everything is cooked and ready.

# Chinese Fried Noodles

350 g fresh rice flour noodles
125 g prawns, shelled
 75 g meat, sliced thinly
 15 fish balls, quartered
 60 g shelled oysters
 95 g spring greens (chye sim)
125 ml water
  2 eggs
  5 small onions, ground coarsely
  2 cloves garlic, ground coarsely
  2 tsps cornflour
1¼ tbsps light soya sauce
 ½ tsp pepper
6½ tbsps oil
Salt to taste

METHOD

1. Combine cornflour, soya sauce, pepper and water.
2. Cut spring greens into 4.5 cm length.
3. Heat oil, saute ground ingredients for 3 minutes over a medium heat.
4. Add meat, prawns, oysters, fish balls, spring greens salt and stir-fry for a while, adding the eggs, stirring well.
5. Add cornflour mixture and when it starts to bubble, add rice noodles and stir, mixing well with all the ingredients.
6. Garnish with omelette strips and chopped spring onions. Serve.

*Burmese Chicken Noodles.*

# Singaporean Laksa

255 g rice noodles, cooked
150 g shelled prawns, cooked
150 g chicken, cooked, shredded
 50 ml peanut oil
 15 ml sesame oil
  1 litre coconut milk
  3 hard boiled eggs, sliced
2½ tsps turmeric powder
  1 tsp coriander seeds, ground
  1 tsp ground ginger
  1 tsp chilli, ground
  1 tsp minced onion
  2 cloves garlic, crushed
  7 peppercorns, ground
Salt to taste

---

METHOD

1. Blend peanut oil and sesame oils together.
2. Saute onion, garlic and gradually add the ground spices.
3. When the ingredients are thoroughly mixed and aromatic, add shrimp paste, stirring for a while over a medium heat.
4. Add coconut milk and salt, allow to simmer until oil appears on the surface. Serve sauce over egg noodles and garnish with cooked chicken, prawns and chopped hard boiled eggs.

# Armenian Lamb Biriani

455 g long grain rice
455 g cooked lamb, diced
750 ml tomato juice
250 ml broth
 50 g dripping/olive oil
  2 tbsps curry powder for meat
  1 tsp freshly ground pepper
 ¼ tsp turmeric powder
 ¼ tsp cinnamon powder
Salt to taste

---

METHOD

1. Brown curry powder in lamb drippings or olive oil over a low heat.
2. Add rice, stir for a couple of minutes, then add in the other ingredients and seasonings, cover and simmer until the rice is cooked.

Note:
For garnish see page 34.

# Indian Fish Biriani

455 g half-cooked long grain rice
500 ml yogurt
  3 red chillies, minced
  4 slices fish (salmon, sea bass)
  3 cloves garlic, crushed
125 g ghee
 15 small onions, minced
  3 tomatoes, sliced
1½ tsps turmeric powder
1½ tsps coriander, ground
1½ tsps garam masala
Pepper and salt to taste

---

METHOD

1. Combine the following ingredients: yogurt, garlic, onions, 1 tsp garam masala, coriander, turmeric and salt.
2. Marinate fish in the combined ingredients for an hour.
3. Heat ghee, fry drained fish till light brown.
4. Later add the marinade and cover with rice, tomatoes, chillies and sprinkle with melted ghee and ½ tsp garam masala.
5. Cover tightly and bake in a 175°C oven for 30 minutes.

Note:
For garnish see page 34.

# Indian Chicken Biriani

455 g long grain Patna rice
500 ml yogurt
455 g chicken, disjointed
500 ml water/broth
  60 g cashew nuts, toasted
  20 small onions, sliced
  70 g raisins, puffed
   7 tbsps oil
   5 cm stick cinnamon
   5 cloves
   2 green chillies, minced
   4 cardamom pods, whole
   6 cloves garlic, mashed
   7 peppercorns, ground
   1 tbsp korma paste (see page 10)
½ tsp turmeric powder
Salt to taste

### METHOD

1. Season yogurt with pepper and salt to make a marinade.
2. Let the chicken stand in the marinade for 1½ hours.
3. Fry the onions and garlic in heated oil until brown.
4. Add drained chicken pieces and stir for a while.
5. Add the remaining spices, seasoning and korma paste; cover the pot for 5 minutes.
6. Add rice, marinade, broth, salt and simmer until all liquid has been absorbed and the rice is dry and fluffy.
7. Mix raisins and cashew nuts thoroughly into the rice.

### Note:
For garnish see page 34.

# Sri Lankan Prawn Biriani

455 g cooked rice
455 g shelled prawns
250 ml curd
   4 small tomatoes, sliced
   3 cloves garlic, minced
   1 sprig curry leaves
  90 g ghee
   2 cloves garlic, ground
   1 tbsp curry powder for fish
  15 cashew nuts, ground
  25 small onions, sliced
   7 cardamom pods
1½ tsps chilli powder
½ tsp turmeric powder
   1 tsp minced ginger
Salt to taste

### METHOD

1. Combine the following ingredients: chilli powder, curry powder, ground cashew nuts, turmeric powder, ground garlic, ginger with the curd.
2. Marinate the prawns in this mixture for 30 minutes.
3. Fry the onions, minced garlic, curry leaves in hot oil for 2 minutes.
4. Add tomatoes, cardamom pods, salt and stir for 5 minutes over a medium heat; then add the prawn mixture.
5. When the gravy is reduced by half, add rice, stir until it is heated through and well-coated.

### Note:
For garnish see page 36

# Basic Pilau

225 g long grain rice
400 ml water/stock
  3 tbsps ghee
½ tsp salt

### METHOD

1. Saute rice in heated ghee on a low heat, stirring continuously until the rice has absorbed the ghee.
2. Add water and bring to the boil for 5 minutes.
3. Reduce the heat, add salt, stir once and cook covered until the rice is cooked and soft.

### Note:
Basmati (Dehra Dun, India) and Patna rice are well-known long grain rice.

# Indian Tomato Pilau

235 g Patna rice
150 ml broth
1 tsp curry powder for vegetable
  3 black peppercorns, crushed
300 ml tomato juice
  3 tbsp vegetable oil
  1 sprig curry leaves
Salt to taste

### METHOD

1. Brown curry leaves and curry powder in heated oil.
2. Stir in the rice for 3 minutes over a low heat.
3. Add in broth, tomato juice, pepper, salt and bring to the boil, then allow to simmer till all liquid is absorbed and the rice cooked.

# Pacific Island Brown Rice Biriani

225 g brown rice
125 g pineapple chunks
125 g orange chunks
100 g walnuts or peanuts roasted, chopped
400 ml pineapple or orange juice
100 ml water
  3 tbsps oil
 ½ tsp ground ginger
  2 small onions, minced
  1 clove garlic, crushed
Pepper and salt to taste

---

### METHOD

1. Saute the onion and garlic in oil until tender.
2. Add water and juice and bring to a boil.
3. Stir in the rice, ginger, pepper and salt, lower the heat and cook until the rice is dry and fluffy.
4. Stir in the pineapple chunks, orange chunks, roasted nuts and when they are heated through, remove.

# Simple Sweet Pilau

455 g Patna rice
100 g ghee
100 g raisins
150 g almonds, blanched
100 g castor sugar
750 ml water
 50 ml melted ghee
100 g pistachios, blanched
  4 cardamom pods
  6 cloves
  5 cm stick cinnamon
  2 blades mace
 ½ tsp saffron/turmeric powder
Pinch of salt
Rose water (flavouring)

---

### METHOD

1. Saute raisins, almonds and pistachios in heated ghee until brown, keep aside.
2. Add rice and brown it lightly over a low heat.
3. Add cardamom pods, cloves, cinnamon, mace, turmeric or saffron, salt, sugar and boiling water.
4. Bring the rice to a boil on a high heat for 5 minutes, then lower the heat, cover until the rice is done.
5. Pour in melted ghee, stir gently and add the fried nuts and raisins. Sprinkle rose water.

*Simple Sweet Pilau.*

# Indian Mutton Biriani

455 g half-cooked Basmati rice
500 ml yogurt
455 g mutton, chopped
 15 cashew nuts, ground
  4 small onions, sliced
  8 peppercorns
  5 cm stick cinnamon
  1 tbsp coriander seeds
  1 tsp cumin seeds
 ½ tsp fennel seeds
  2 tsps poppy seeds
 ½ tsp grated nutmeg
  1 tbsp lemon juice
1½ tsps minced ginger
Salt to taste

**METHOD**

1. Grind coriander seeds, cumin seeds, poppy seeds, peppercorns, and fennel seeds.
2. Grind ginger, mix it with the lemon juice.
3. Rub the ginger mixture into the mutton pieces, allowing to marinate for half hour.
4. Then add the seasonings, whole and ground spices, ground cashew nuts, nutmeg, onion and curd or yogurt to the mutton.
5. Cook covered with a tight fitting lid and simmer for 45 minutes.
6. Add partially cooked rice and mix thoroughly; replace lid and simmer for another 15 – 20 minutes.

Note:
For garnish see page 34.

*Indian Mutton Biriani.*

# Middle East Oyster Pilau

250 g long grain rice
200 g shelled oysters
200 g shelled mussels
125 g olive oil
500 ml water
 ¼ tsp pepper
 ½ tsp parsley and dill herbs
 7 small onions, minced
Salt to taste

---

METHOD

1.   Brown onions in heated olive oil.
2.   Add water and bring to a boil.
3.   Add rice, oysters, mussels, herbs, pepper and salt.
4.   Simmer briskly till moisture has evaporated, then place in a pre-heated oven for a few minutes. Remove.

# Indian Prawn Pilau

250 g long grain rice
 75 g ghee
100 g almonds, roasted, slivered
 2 small onions, sliced
 1 clove garlic, crushed
 ½ tsp chilli powder
 1 tsp mixed spices (see page 6)
500 ml boiling water
455 g shelled prawns
225 ml curd
 1 tbsp curry powder for fish
 ½ tsp turmeric powder
Salt to taste

---

METHOD

1.   Wash, soak and drain the rice after 45 minutes.
2.   Fry the onions, garlic in heated ghee, then add rice, salt and stir for a few minutes over a medium heat.
3.   Turn the heat low, then add water, cover and cook until the rice is dry.
4.   In the meantime, rub chilli powder, turmeric powder and salt to the prawns.
5.   Heat the remaining ghee, toss the prawns until partially cooked.
6.   Add curry powder, mixed spices, curd and cook it with the lid on over a slow fire until the gravy is three quarters reduced.
7.   Add the rice and slivered almonds and stir until the rice is well mixed with all the ingredients.

*Middle East Oyster Pilau.*

# Eggs

*"There is no love sincerer than the love of food."*
— *George Bernard Shaw*

# Basic Egg Curry

    7 hard-boiled eggs, shelled
250 ml yogurt
    1 large onion, minced
    1 tbsp ghee
½ tsp freshly ground black pepper
    1 tsp fresh turmeric, ground
    1 tsp chilli powder
    1 tsp lime juice
½ tsp fresh ginger, ground
Salt to taste

---

METHOD

1.  Saute onion; then add ginger, turmeric, pepper, chilli, salt and stir for 2 minutes.
2.  Now add the following ingredients: yogurt, eggs and lime juice.
3.  Simmer covered over a very low heat for 45 minutes.

# Basic Curried Eggs

    6 hard-boiled eggs, shelled
275 ml curry sauce (see page 18)
    1 tbsp grated red chilli
Chopped parsley and coriander leaves
1 small lemon, wedged

---

METHOD

1.  Heat the sauce and allow to simmer for 30 minutes over a very low heat.
2.  Add eggs and cook until eggs are heated through.
3.  Dish and garnish with chopped parsley and lemon. Sprinkle chilli.

# Hawaiian Steamed Eggs

    7 eggs, beaten
20 medium-sized prawns, shelled
Pinch of saffron
¼ tsp soya sauce
½ tsp pepper
    2 tbsps water
Salt to taste

---

METHOD

1.  Mix all the ingredients and steam until the eggs are set.

# Chinese Scrambled Eggs

    7 egg whites
200 g cooked prawns, shelled
    4 tbsps oil
    1 tbsp sherry
1½ tsps grated ginger
    1 tbsp light soya sauce
½ tsp pepper
Salt to taste

---

METHOD

1.  Beat the egg whites with salt until stiff.
2.  Fold in the soya sauce, pepper, ginger, prawns and sherry.
3.  Pour the mixture on heated oil, stirring constantly until well scrambled.

# Indian Moolie Egg Curry

    7 eggs
250 ml coconut milk, thick
    40 g ghee
    4 red chillies, sliced lengthways
    2 cloves garlic, crushed
    1 sprig coriander leaves or curry leaves
    2 small onions, sliced
½ tsp ginger, minced
½ tsp turmeric powder
    1 tbsp vinegar
Salt to taste

---

METHOD

1.  Bring eggs to the boil with vinegar and then shell.
2.  Fry the following ingredients in hot ghee: onions, garlic, ginger, chillies, curry leaves or coriander leaves and stir for a minute or two.
3.  Add coconut milk, turmeric powder, eggs and salt to taste. Turn the heat to low and simmer uncovered until the mixture is thick.

# Pakistani Egg Curry

7 hard-boiled eggs, shelled
5 medium-sized potatoes, sliced
2 small onions, sliced
2 cardamom pods, crushed
225 ml yogurt
150 g ghee
½ tsp turmeric powder
½ tsp curry powder
½ tsp ground ginger
½ tsp chilli powder
2½ tsps ground coriander
Salt to taste

---

METHOD

1. Saute onions lightly and then add potatoes, ground and powdered spices, stirring until the colour changes or for approximately 7 – 10 minutes.
2. Add eggs, cardamom pods and salt. Stir for a minute or two.
3. Add yogurt and simmer covered until the gravy is well mixed and rather thick.

# Indian Egg Curry with Lentils

7 hard-boiled eggs, shelled, halved
125 g lentils
4 small onions, sliced
3 red chillies, sliced
65 g ghee
1½ tbsps curry powder for fish
½ tsp chilli powder
125 ml hot water
Salt to taste

---

METHOD

1. Soak the lentils overnight, drain.
2. Fry the onions and chillies until brown.
3. Add the curry powder, chilli powder and lentils.
4. Cook the lentils for 3 minutes and then add hot water.
5. Season with salt and when the lentils are tender, add the eggs just a few minutes before removing the lentil curry from the fire.

*Indian Egg Curry with Lentils.*

# Sri Lankan Egg Curry with Dried Fish

    7 hard-boiled eggs, shelled
120 g dried fish, sliced
250 ml stock
    4 tomatoes, quartered
    1 sprig curry leaves
Oil
    1 tbsp fish curry powder
½ tsp turmeric powder
½ tsp ginger, ground
    4 dried chillies, ground
250 ml coconut, ground
    7 cloves garlic, ground
    8 small onions, ground
    7 peppercorns, ground
Salt to taste

---

METHOD

1.  Heat three tablespoons oil, fry dried fish and then add ground ingredients and fry until it gives out an aroma
2.  Blend coconut, turmeric, curry powder, salt and add to the pan, stirring well.
3.  Add eggs, tomatoes and curry leaves and simmer uncovered until gravy dries up.

# Malaysian Omelette

    4 eggs
15 small prawns, shelled
    3 red chillies, pounded
    5 small onions, pounded
½ tsp shrimp paste, roasted
    1 tbsp spring onion, chopped
Oil
Salt to taste

GARNISH
    2 red chillies, shredded
    3 tbsps coriander leaves

---

METHOD

1.  Beat eggs with a pinch of salt.
2.  Heat 3 tablespoons oil, saute chilli, and onion pastes until fragrant.
3.  Add prawns and fry for two minutes.
4.  Then add spring onion and stir for a minute.
5.  Spread the mixture well and then pour in the beaten eggs. When it is set and cooked, roll it up loosely and dish onto a platter.
6.  Garnish with shredded chillies and coriander leaves.

# Indonesian Spicy Egg Curry

    7 hard-boiled eggs, shelled
250 ml coconut milk, thick
  20 small onions, minced
    4 cloves garlic, minced
    2 cm lemon grass, sliced
Oil
    1 tsp chilli powder
    1 tsp shrimp paste
    1 tsp grated lemon rind
½ tsp sugar
    1 tbsp soya sauce
Salt to taste

---

METHOD

1.  Brown eggs in moderately heated oil, remove.
2.  Pound the following ingredients: onions, garlic, shrimp paste, lemon grass, lemon rind, sugar, salt and chilli powder.
3.  Add this mixture to a heated pan with three table-spoons oil, stirring frequently to prevent burning.
4.  When the spices are well browned and aromatic, add soya sauce, coconut milk and eggs.
5.  Cook over a low heat until a thick sauce is formed.

# Indonesian Omelette

    5 eggs, beaten
    1 spring onion, chopped
Peanut oil
½ tsp chilli paste
½ tsp roasted prawn paste
½ tsp salt

GARNISH
    2 red chillies, shredded
    3 tbsps coriander leaves

---

METHOD

1.  Soften shrimp paste in a teaspoon of water.
2.  Combine the eggs, chilli paste, shrimp paste, onion and salt.
3.  Heat oil, pour the egg mixture and fry on both sides. Cut into wide strips.
4.  Garnish with shredded chillies and coriander leaves.

# Indonesian Egg Curry with Prawns

    7 hard-boiled eggs, shelled
250 ml coconut milk, thick
225 g dried prawns, soaked, pounded
    5 red chillies, ground
¼ tsp turmeric, ground
  15 small onions, ground
    2 green chillies, ground
½ tsp ground ginger
    1 tbsp tamarind water
Oil
Salt to taste

## METHOD

1.  Heat four tablespoons oil and brown eggs. Remove eggs from pan.
2.  Add ground ingredients, pounded prawns and fry till fragrant.
3.  Add milk, tamarind water, eggs and salt. Allow to simmer uncovered on a low heat until the oil comes to the surface.

# Singaporean Egg Fried with Shredded Cabbage

450 g cabbage, shredded
  15 medium sized prawns, shelled, diced
    3 red chillies, sliced
    4 eggs, well beaten
    2 cloves garlic, crushed
½ tsp chilli paste
    3 tbsps oil
Salt to taste

## METHOD

1.  Heat oil, add garlic and red chillies and fry until brown.
2.  Add chilli paste, prawns, salt and stir for two minutes.
3.  Add cabbage, stir well, cover pan and cook for 7 minutes.
4.  Stir then add eggs. Continue stirring gently until egg hardens.

# Singaporean Steamed Eggs

    4 eggs, beaten
125 ml coconut milk, thick
¼ tsp curry powder
½ tsp chilli powder
    2 tbsps butter
Salt to taste

## METHOD

1.  Blend milk, butter, curry powder, chilli powder, salt with eggs.
2.  Whisk in a bowl, then steam mixture in a pot with a tight fitting lid until cooked.

# Singaporean Eggs with Spinach

    4 eggs, beaten
125 g spinach, chopped
Oil
½ tsp curry powder
Pepper/salt to taste

## METHOD

1.  Fry the spinach briskly in heated oil for a couple of minutes.
2   Remove the spinach and combine it with the eggs, curry powder, pepper and salt.
3.  Heat pan with oil smeared on it, pour the egg mixture and cook until set.

# Malaysian Stuffed Egg

    6 hard-boiled eggs, shelled
    3 red chillies, pounded
  60 ml coconut milk, thick
    3 small tomatoes
    3 small onions, pounded
½ tsp shrimp paste, roasted, pounded
    1 sprig coriander leaves
Salt to taste
Oil

## METHOD

1.  Cut the tomatoes into halves and remove the pulp. Chop the pulp up.
2.  Pound the chillies, onions and shrimp paste well.
3.  Heat oil, fry the pounded ingredients until fragrant.
4.  Then add tomato pulp, coconut milk and salt.
5.  When it is cooked, remove and cool.
6.  Slice the top off the eggs, remove the yolks and mash with the cooked ingredients.
7.  Fill the eggs with the mixture. Stand the eggs on tomato halves and garnish with coriander leaves.

# British Curried Eggs

   7 hard-boiled eggs, shelled, halved
   1 small onion, chopped
250 ml stock/ water
 35 g butter
 10 g ginger, minced
  1 sprig parsley, chopped
  1 tbsp fish curry powder, mild
  1 tbsp flour
  1 tbsp vinegar
  2 tbsps tomato puree
1½ tbsps chutney
Pepper and salt to taste

---

METHOD

1. Saute onion until soft.
2. Add ginger, curry powder and flour and cook for 2 minutes.
3. Add tomato puree, vinegar and chutney, stir well.
4. Add stock, pepper and salt.
5. Bring to a boil and then simmer over a low heat until it thickens.
6. Add eggs and when they are well heated through, remove.
7. Garnish with parsley.

# British Peppered Eggs with Potatoes

 7 eggs
 5 large potatoes
 7 tbsps butter
 1 sprig parsley
 7 tbsps milk
2 tsps pepper
¼ tsp cinnamon powder
Salt to taste

---

METHOD

1. Boil, skin and mash potatoes with butter, heated milk, 1 tsp pepper and salt.
2. Spread the creamed potatoes in an oven proof dish.
3. Make seven depressions on the surface and break an egg into each depression.
4. Sprinkle the remaining pepper and salt on the eggs.
5. Bake in a medium heat oven until the eggs are set.
6. Sprinkle cinnamon powder on top after removing from the oven.
7. Garnish with parsley.

*British Peppered Eggs with Potatoes.*

*Jaffna Poached Egg Curry.*

# Jaffna Poached Egg Curry

  7 eggs
500 ml coconut milk
  1 large onion, sliced
  2 green chillies, sliced
  1 sprig curry leaves
  2 tbsps fish curry powder
¼ tsp cumin, crushed
½ tsp black peppercorns, ground
½ tsp garlic paste
Lime juice and salt to taste

---

METHOD

1. Combine the following ingredients: coconut milk, onion, chillies, curry leaves, curry powder, cumin, pepper, garlic paste and salt.
2. Bring to a boil, then allow to simmer over a low heat until gravy thickens.
3. Break an egg into the boiling liquid, stir the gravy as the egg cooks. Do not break yolk. Repeat this method for the remaining eggs.
4. Squeeze in lime juice before serving.

# Nepalese Omelette

  5 eggs, beaten
  3 red chillies, de-seeded, sliced
  1 small onion, sliced
½ tsp ginger, minced
  1 tbsp coriander leaves
  3 tbsps ghee
Salt to taste

GARNISH
  2 red chillies, shredded
  3 tbsps coriander leaves

---

METHOD

1. Saute onions and chillies in melted ghee.
2. Remove the sauted ingredients and mix with eggs, ginger, coriander leaves and salt.
3. Fry an omelette with the mixture.
4. Garnish with shredded chillies and coriander leaves.

# Indian Egg Curry With Eggplant

7 hard-boiled eggs, shelled
1 medium-sized eggplant, sliced
10 small onions, sliced
2 cloves garlic, crushed
250 ml coconut milk, thick
Juice of a small lime
1 tbsp curry powder
1 tsp tomato paste
½ tsp chilli powder
4 tbsps ghee
Salt to taste

### METHOD

1. Fry sliced eggplant in ghee. When the eggplant becomes brown, add onions and garlic.
2. Then combine coconut milk, curry powder, chilli powder, tomato paste, salt and cook the mixture on a low heat for 15 minutes, stirring well.
3. Add the eggs, lime juice and simmer covered until eggs are heated through.

# Indian Spiced Egg Curry

7 hard-boiled eggs, shelled
250 ml coconut milk, thick
3 small onions, ground
2 cloves garlic, crushed
2 red chillies, sliced
1 sprig curry leaves
1½ tsps ground cumin
2 tsps ground coriander
½ tsp grated ginger
½ tsp curry powder for egg
2 tbsps oil
Salt to taste

### METHOD

1. Combine ground ingredients, garlic, curry powder and salt.
2. Fry the combined ingredients in heated oil, stirring all the time for 5 – 7 minutes or until it gives out an aroma.
3. Add eggs, coconut milk, curry leaves, ginger and chillies.
4. Turn the heat to moderate, simmer uncovered until mixture thickens.

# Indian Egg Curry with Onions

5 hard-boiled eggs, shelled
450 g small onions, sliced
4 tbsps ghee
2 tbsps tamarind concentrate
3 tbsps coriander leaves
250 ml water
½ tsp chilli powder
½ tsp garlic paste
1 tsp ginger paste
Salt to taste

### METHOD

1. Make incisions in the hard-boiled eggs.
2. Heat the ghee and cook over a medium heat the onions, chilli powder, garlic and ginger pastes until the onions become transparent.
3. Sprinkle a little water if necessary. Then add the tamarind concentrate dissolved in water.
4. Add eggs and salt and cook until the gravy thickens and the oil comes to the surface.
5. Sprinkle coriander leaves.

# Indian Poached Eggs

2 eggs
250 ml stock or water
1½ tsps fish curry powder
Pepper and salt to taste

### METHOD

1. Combine curry powder, pepper, salt in water or stock and bring the liquid to a boil.
2. Break an egg into the boiling water or stock, poach to your taste.
3. Stir the liquid as the egg cooks. Repeat method with remaining eggs.

# Jaffna Omelette Curry

   4 eggs
450 ml coconut milk
100 g small onions, sliced
  70 g ghee
    5 red chillies, sliced
    1 sprig curry leaves
    1 tbsp chilli powder
    2 tsps coriander seeds, roasted, ground
¼ tsp cumin seeds, roasted, ground
½ tsp black peppercorns, ground
¼ tsp turmeric powder
¼ garlic paste
Lime juice and salt to taste

### METHOD

1. Beat the eggs and add a tablespoon onion, 1 red chilli and salt.
2. Heat a little ghee; pour in the eggs and allow to set.
3. When completely set, turn omelette over and fry for a a while. Remove and cut into equal, small pieces.
4. Now heat the remaining ghee, add onions and fry until light brown.
5. Add red chillies, garlic paste, chilli powder, curry leaves, spices, salt and stir for 3 minutes.
6. Add coconut milk and allow to simmer until the gravy reduces and thickens.
7. Now add the omelette pieces and allow to heat through.
8. Squeeze in lime juice to taste just before serving.

# Moroccan Scrambled Eggs

   7 eggs, beaten
   2 small tomatoes, chopped
   2 small onions, chopped
Coriander leaves
½ tsp paprika or chilli powder
   2 tbsps butter
   1 clove garlic, crushed
Pepper and salt to taste

### METHOD

1. Saute onions and garlic in butter until tender.
2. Add tomatoes, pepper, chilli or paprika powder, salt and stir until the mixture is thoroughly cooked.
3. Add beaten eggs, sprinkle with coriander leaves and scramble gently over a low heat.

# Seafood

*"The stomach supports the heart, and not the heart the stomach."*

— *Old English Proverb*

# Basic Fish Curry for Beginners

2 slices white fish, 1.5 cm thick
1 tbsp mustard oil
1 large onion
200 ml coconut milk
1½ tsps curry powder for seafood
Lime juice and salt to taste

### METHOD

1. Heat oil, fry the onion until soft.
2. Then add curry powder and fry until it begins to change colour.
3. Add coconut milk, bring to the boil, then lower the heat, add fish fillets, salt and cook uncovered until fish is done.
4. Squeeze in lime juice before serving.

# Basic Curried Fish

2 slices white fish, 1.5 cm thick
1 tsp parsley
1 tsp de-seeded chilli, minced
250 ml curry sauce (see page 18)
Lemon juice to taste

### METHOD

1. Make curry sauce and simmer for 30 minutes over a very low heat.
2. Add in fish fillets and heat carefully in the sauce until cooked.
3. Sprinkle parsley, chilli and add lemon juice before serving.

# Indian Fish with Almond Sauce

450 g white fish, cleaned
200 g almonds, ground
3 small onions, sliced, ground
4 peppercorns, freshly ground
Mustard oil
250 ml water
1 tsp turmeric powder
1 tsp garam masala
1 tsp minced ginger, ground
1 sprig curry leaves
Salt to taste

### METHOD

1. Combine some of the almond paste, onion and ginger together with a little water.
2. Cut the fish into 1.5 cm pieces, smear with almond paste and deep fry in heated oil. Keep it aside.
3. Remove oil, leaving three tablespoons in pan; then add turmeric powder, pepper, garam masala, curry leaves, salt, water and the remaining almond paste.
4. When it boils and thickens, remove and pour it over the fish. Serve hot.

# Indian Steamed Fish Curry

450 g white fish
125 g tomatoes, chopped
2 green chillies, slit lengthwise
2 red chillies, slit lengthwise
5 tbsps mustard oil
¼ tsp sugar
1 sprig curry leaves
1 tsp cumin seeds, ground
1 tsp minced ginger, ground
1 small onion, ground
¼ tsp fenugreek seeds, ground
½ tsp turmeric powder
1 tsp pepper, freshly ground
Salt to taste

### METHOD

1. Clean, cut fish into cubes, drain.
2. Mix all the ingredients together with the fish in a pan with a close fitting lid and steam until fish is cooked.
3. Serve hot with rice.

Note:
For garnish see page 34.

# Indian Fish Head Curry

150 g fish head
250 ml coconut milk, thick
125 ml coconut milk, thin
  2 small onions, ground
  2 small onions, sliced
  4 cloves garlic, ground
Oil
  1 tsp chilli powder
  1 tsp turmeric powder
  1 tsp minced ginger, ground
  3 green chillies, sliced
  1 tsp garam masala
  1 sprig curry leaves
Salt to taste

### METHOD

1. Fry the fish head in oil and keep aside.
2. Fry the sliced onions until soft, add ground and powdered ingredients and fry till fragrant.
3. Add thin coconut milk and allow to simmer until gravy reduces by half, then add a sprig of curry leaves and salt, stirring for a while.
4. Add thick coconut milk and bring to a boil. Then add fish head and allow to simmer uncovered until the gravy becomes thick and the fish is ready to be served.

Note:
For garnish see page 34

# Mauritius Fish Curry

  1 pomfret, cleaned
250 ml water
  ½ tsp lime juice
  2 cloves garlic, ground
  4 small onions, ground
10 fresh chillies, ground
  ½ tsp curry paste for seafood
Salt to taste

### METHOD

1. Cut fish into suitable pieces.
2. Combine the ground ingredients with salt and water, simmer over a low heat.
3. When the gravy begins to boil, add in the fish. Keep turning until it is cooked.
4. Sprinkle lime juice just before removing pan from the fire.

# Northern African Fish Curry

225 g cooked fish
250 ml water
  70 g butter
  2 small onions
Pinch of turmeric powder
  1 apple
  6 cm stick rhubarb
  1 tbsp flour
  1 tbsp curry powder
  1 tbsp lemon juice
Pepper and salt to taste

### METHOD

1. Mix the following ingredients together: curry powder, flour, lemon juice, water, pepper and salt.
2. Remove skin and bones of fish. Flake.
3. Peel and cut apple, rhubarb and onions rather thickly.
4. Brown apple, rhubarb, onion in moderately hot butter.
5. Add in mixed ingredients, stir, bring to a boil on a high heat for 3 minutes, then turn the heat low to simmer.
6. When the gravy has reduced by half, add in the fish, stirring well for a couple of minutes before removing.

# Indonesian Fish Stew

  1 whole fish (mackerel)
  4 small onions, ground
  4 candlenuts, ground
  ¼ tsp fresh ginger, ground
  8 dried red chillies, ground
  3 cloves garlic, ground
  ¼ tsp turmeric, ground
  3 basil leaves, chopped, bruised
Salt to taste

### METHOD

1. Mix the ground ingredients together.
2. Smear the cleaned, dried fish with ground paste.
3. Put fish in a pan with remaining ground paste, salt, basil leaves and pour in enough water to cover the fish. Simmer uncovered on a very low heat until the fish is cooked.

Note:
For garnish see page 36

# Indian Stuffed Crab Meat in Shells

300 g crab meat, cooked
100 g cooked potatoes, cut into small cubes
   2 eggs, well beaten
125 ml stock from crab legs
Melted ghee or butter
   2 tbsps ghee
   1 tbsp coriander leaves, chopped
   2 small onions, minced
   6 dried chillies, ground
   3 cloves, ground
   2 cm sticks cinnamon, ground
 50 g coconut, ground
   6 cloves garlic, ground
10 peppercorns, ground
¼ tsp minced ginger, ground
Salt to taste
Breadcrumbs
Lemon juice to taste

## METHOD

1. Heat ghee, fry onions until light brown.
2. Then add ground ingredients stirring constantly for a few minutes.
3. Add potatoes, crab meat, salt and coriander leaves, stirring until well mixed.
4. Then add stock, cover and allow to simmer until nearly cooked.
5. Add eggs, scramble well into the crab mixture until set.
6. Wash, dry four large shells then fill with the crab mixture, sprinkle with breadcrumbs and a few drops of lemon juice and a little ghee or butter.
7. Place these shells in pre-heated oven for 3 – 4 minutes before serving.

*Indian Stuffed Crab Meat in Shells.*

*Singaporean Sardine Curry.*

# Vietnamese Fried Crabs

6 small crabs, cleaned
1 tsp garlic powder
1 tbsp pepper, ground
Peanut oil
Salt to taste

## METHOD

1. Pound the crab quarters lightly to crack the shells.
2. Mix the crabs with garlic, pepper and salt, allowing to marinate for 3 – 4 hours.
3. Heat oil and fry till cooked.

# Singaporean Sardine Curry

455 g tinned sardines or mackerel
4 medium sized tomatoes, chopped
3 cloves garlic, ground
150 ml coconut milk, thick
1 sprig curry leaves
2 tsps curry paste for fish
3 green chillies, sliced
1 large onion, sliced
Salt to taste
Oil

## METHOD

1. Heat oil, fry onions, garlic, chillies and curry leaves until tender.
2. Add tomatoes, curry paste, coconut milk and salt, allow to simmer for 20 minutes.
3. Add sardines and cook until the mixture is well blended and the sardine is well heated.

# Greek Fish Curry

225 g cod
225 g tomatoes, chopped
70 ml water
1 large onion, chopped
4 tbsps oil
1 tsp fresh dill
½ tsp curry powder for seafood
¼ tsp sugar
1 stalk celery, chopped
Lemon juice, pepper and salt to taste

METHOD

1. Clean and cut fish into fillets.
2. Saute onions in heated oil lightly, then add tomatoes, celery, dill, water, pepper, sugar, salt and curry powder.
3. Cover pan and cook over a moderately low heat until the sauce has thickened.
4. Add fish fillets, cook until tender. Add lemon juice before removing.

# Iraqi Sweet and Sour Baked Fish Curry

455 g white fish
60 ml lemon juice
1 large tomato, sliced thinly
1 large onion, sliced
Oil
2 tbsps flour
2 tbsps brown sugar
¼ tsp turmeric powder
½ tsp curry powder for seafood
Pinch of cumin powder
Salt to taste

METHOD

1. Cut fish into serving pieces, clean, dry before dredging lightly with flour.
2. Fry the fish in heated oil, until done. Remove and arrange on an ovenproof dish.
3. Saute onion in a tablespoon of oil, then add turmeric powder, cumin powder, salt and cook over a low heat until well mixed.
4. Pour this mixture over the fish, then arrange the sliced tomatoes and then sprinkle curry powder mixed with lemon juice.
5. Bake it for 15 minutes over a medium heat, then sprinkle sugar on top. Bake again until most of the liquid has been absorbed by the fish.

# Bangladesh Fish Yogurt Curry

455 g cod
280 ml yogurt
40 g ghee
2 green chillies, sliced
½ tsp ground turmeric
¼ tsp sugar
1 clove garlic, crushed
1 small onion, sliced
1 tsp garam masala
1 tsp ground ginger
½ tsp chilli powder
Salt to taste

METHOD

1. Blend yogurt with turmeric, ginger, chilli powder and salt.
2. Cut fish into suitable pieces and allow to marinate in the blended ingredients for an hour.
3. Saute onion, chillies and garlic in heated ghee until tender.
4. Stir in the garam masala and sugar.
5. When the ingredients are well mixed, add in the fish mixture, simmer covered for ten minutes or until fish is tender.

# Indo-Chinese Fish with Anise Sauce

455 g fillet (white fish)
Flour
20 small onions, minced
4 cloves garlic, minced
300 ml water
1 tsp ground anise
1 tsp chilli powder
2 tbsps vinegar
2 tsps sugar
2 tsps shrimp paste/fish sauce
Pinch of pepper
Oil

METHOD

1. Cut the fish into bite sized pieces; dredge with the flour, and deep fry in heated oil. Keep fish aside.
2. Remove remaining oil, leaving enough to fry onions. Fry onions and then add garlic, anise, chilli powder, vinegar, sugar and water.
3. Cook over a low heat for 10 minutes, then add in fish sauce or shrimp paste and pepper.
4. Put the fish in the same, cook until fish is well heated.

# Indian Fish Vindaloo

455 g fish, sliced
250 ml water
  2 small onions, sliced
  2 green chillies, sliced
  4 small tomatoes, sliced
  ½ tsp garam masala
  1 tsp brown sugar
  1 tsp turmeric, ground
1½ tsps ginger, ground
  1 tsp mustard seeds, ground
  ½ tsp cumin seeds, ground
  7 red chillies, ground
  8 cloves garlic, ground
  4 peppercorns, ground
Salt to taste
Vinegar
Oil

### METHOD

1. Grind ingredients with vinegar only.
2. Heat oil, fry onions, chillies, ground ingredients, stirring well for 5 minutes over a medium heat.
3. Add tomatoes, water and sugar.
4. When it comes to a boil, add garam masala, salt and preferably white fish or salmon, simmer until fish is cooked.

# English Curried Cod

225 g cod, cleaned
 70 g butter
Lemon juice to taste
  1 tsp curry powder for fish
  1 tbsp flour
Pepper and salt to taste
  1 medium-sized lemon
Sprig of parsley

### METHOD

1. Cut cod into finger lengths and place in a greased casserole.
2. Heat butter, stir in the curry powder, pepper, salt and gradually add in the flour.
3. When the curry powder has changed colour, pour it over the fish and bake in a medium heat until the fish is done. Serve hot with a sprinkling of lemon juice.
4. Slice lemon thinly. Remove pips, serrate edge and cut into quarters.
5. Garnish with lemon quarters in butterfly shapes and parsley.

# Brazilian White Fish Curry

225 g white fish, cooked, flaked
250 ml coconut milk
  2 tomatoes, peeled, chopped
  2 small onions, minced
Oil
 10 coriander seeds, ground
  4 peppercorns, ground
  1 clove garlic, ground
Juice of ½ lemon
Salt to taste

### METHOD

1. Fry onions in heated oil until brown.
2. Then add tomatoes, coconut milk, ground spices, salt and stir over a moderate heat.
3. When it reaches a thick consistency, add fish, stirring for a couple of minutes until the fish is heated thoroughly.
4. Add lemon juice before serving.

# Malay Barbecued Fish

  1 small fish, cleaned
  2 cloves garlic, minced
50 ml coconut milk, thick
  ¼ tsp ginger, ground
  1 small onion, minced
  3 red chillies, minced
Juice of ½ lemon (to taste)
Pinch of salt

### METHOD

1. Combine the following ingredients together: onion, chillies, garlic, ginger, coconut milk and a pinch of salt.
2. Make a few vertical cuts in the cleaned fish.
3. Marinate the fish in the combined ingredients for 5 – 6 hours.
4. Grill it basting frequently with the marinade until done and serve with lemon juice.

Note:
It can be grilled over a charcoal fire or under an oven grill.

# Singaporean Lobster Curry

455 g lobster meat
255 g tomatoes, chopped
120 g small onions, chopped
250 ml coconut milk, thick
    2 cucumbers, peeled, cubed
    1 red chilli, sliced
    2 cloves garlic, minced
    1 sprig curry leaves
    3 tbsps curry powder for seafood
    7 tbsps butter
1½ tsps ginger powder
    1 tbsp cornstarch
    2 tbsps almond powder
    1 tbsp lemon juice
    1 tsp sugar
Salt to taste

## METHOD

1. Saute onion and garlic in melted butter until lightly browned.
2. Stir in the curry leaves, ginger, almond powder, curry powder and salt. Add the tomatoes later.
3. Cover and cook over low heat for 5 minutes. Sprinkle with cornstarch and gradually add the coconut milk, stirring constantly until thickened.
4. Add lobster, cook over low heat for 10 minutes, then add cucumber, red chilli, lemon juice and sugar; cook for 3 minutes.

# Indian Oyster Curry

300 g oyster, shelled
250 ml coconut milk, thick
    5 small onions, sliced
    3 green chillies, sliced
    2 tsps curry powder for seafood
    ½ tsp chilli powder
    2 cloves garlic, crushed
Lemon juice and salt to taste

## METHOD

1. Open the oyster carefully to preserve as much of the liquid as possible, discarding the shells.
2. Combine all the ingredients and simmer covered over a very low fire. Remove when liquid has nearly reduced and oysters are cooked.

*Singaporean Lobster Curry.*

# British Baked Cuttlefish Curry

7 large sized cuttlefish, cleaned
2 cloves garlic, crushed
Parsley
Butter or olive oil
¼ tsp curry powder for fish
Juice of a lemon
Pepper and salt to taste

---

METHOD

1.  Place cleaned cuttlefish with olive oil or butter in pan. Bake, turning once.
2.  Remove the cuttlefish from the pan. Drain the liquid and season cuttlefish with pepper, salt and sprinkle with curry powder, garlic and parsley. Bake again for another 30 minutes.
3.  Turn the heat to low for the last 15 minutes. Sprinkle lemon juice to taste before serving.

# Malay Stuffed Cuttlefish

200 g small cuttlefish
150 g minced meat
 50 g minced prawns
150 ml tamarind water
200 ml water
   5 candlenuts, ground
  12 small onions, ground
   8 red chillies, ground
   5 dried chillies, ground
   1 tsp shrimp paste, ground
Sugar, pepper and salt to taste
Oil

---

METHOD

1.  Clean, wash the cuttlefish with salt, drain, dry. Separate the heads and discard the eyes.
2.  Mix minced meat, prawns, salt and pepper and use it to stuff the cuttlefish.
3.  Reposition the head into place and fasten with toothpicks.
4.  Heat two tablespoons oil, fry ground ingredients for 3 – 4 minutes.
5.  Add tamarind water, water, salt, pepper and sugar and bring to a boil.
6.  Add cuttlefish, lower the heat to medium and cook 10 – 15 minutes. Stir. Do not overcook cuttlefish. Cover and cook for the last 3 minutes on a low heat.

# Malay Steamed Fish

550 g fish, cooked, flaked
125 ml coconut milk, thick
   1 stalk lemon grass, pounded
   1 tsp minced turmeric, pounded
   3 eggs
Pieces of banana leaf
   6 dried chillies, pounded
   6 small onions, pounded
   1 clove garlic, pounded
   4 tbsps coriander seeds, pounded
   4 tbsps cumin seeds, pounded
Salt to taste

---

METHOD

1.  Mix the following ingredients and spices together: mashed fish, pounded and ground ingredients, coconut milk, eggs and salt.
2.  When the mixture is well mixed, divide into required and equal portions.
3.  Put each portion on a piece of banana leaf of 25 cm x 20 cm which has been browned lightly over fire. Bring sides of banana leaf up and fasten with a toothpick to make package.
4.  Place packages in a pot and steam for 20 – 30 minutes or until done.

Note:
Aluminium foil or parchment paper can be used instead of banana leaf. Cut pieces of foil 24 cm x 16 cm. Lightly oil them, then place some of the mixture in the centre of each; fold over into envelope-shaped packages and arrange on a greased baking sheet. Bake in a 350°F oven for 40 minutes or until done. Slit the edges and serve. You can also steam them. This recipe is known throughout S.E. Asia by various names.

# Indonesian Fish Curry

250 g fish fillets (grey mullet)
125 ml coconut milk, thick
125 ml coconut milk, thin
  5 small onions, ground
  2 cloves garlic, ground
  1 stalk lemon grass, ground
  3 candlenuts, ground
Tamarind Juice
  2 tbsps coriander seeds, ground
  7 dried chillies, ground
  1 tsp fennel seeds, ground
½ tsp cumin seeds, ground
½ tsp ground turmeric
  1 tsp ground ginger
Salt to taste

METHOD

1. Blend thin coconut milk with ground ingredients.
2. Bring it to a boil, stirring in the thick coconut milk, tamarind juice and salt.
3. When it begins to bubble, add fish. Cover the pot and continue to cook until the fish is ready to be served.

Note:
For garnish see page 36

# Indian Fish Curry

225 g white fish
350 ml curd
  5 green chillies, sliced lengthwise
  1 large onion, sliced
  4 dried red chillies, ground
  1 tsp turmeric powder
½ tsp curry powder
  2 tsps garam masala
  1 tsp ground ginger
  1 tbsp coriander leaves
Salt to taste

METHOD

1. Clean, cut fish into 4 cm pieces and then rub with turmeric powder, ginger and salt.
2. Combine fish, curd and green chillies and marinate in a covered bowl for 30 minutes.
3. Saute onion and then add garam masala, curry powder in heated ghee, stirring well, adding ground chillies.
4. Add fish mixture, simmer covered until gravy is thick.
5. Sprinkle coriander leaves before removing pan from the fire.

# Sri Lanka Salted Fish Curry

5.4 cm pieces salted fish
  4 small eggplants, quartered
  4 green chillies, sliced
  7 dried chillies, ground
125 ml coconut milk, thick
  1 sprig curry leaves
40 g coconut, ground
  4 cloves garlic, crushed
  9 small onions, sliced
  1 tsp cumin seeds, ground
¼ tsp minced turmeric, ground
  1 tbsp coriander seeds, ground
  1 tbsp tamarind water
Oil
Salt to taste

METHOD

1. Fry the onions, garlic, green chillies, eggplants and curry leaves until tender.
2. Remove excess oil, add ground ingredients in two tablespoons oil and stir for a few minutes until fragrant.
3. Add coconut milk, salted fish, tamarind water and salt and allow to cook over a low heat until it thickens.

Note:
As the fish is salted, the amount of salt added should be controlled carefully.

# Sri Lanka Fish Cutlets

300 g white fish
  2 egg whites
  2 egg yolks
  4 green chillies, minced
  1 large onion, minced
  1 sprig curry leaves
Breadcrumbs
Salt to taste
Oil

METHOD

1. Boil fish, remove bones and mix it throughly with onion, chillies, curry leaves, egg yolks and salt.
2. Form the mixture into small cutlets and coat with egg whites.
3. Sprinkle with breadcrumbs. Deep fry in heated oil until brown.

# Tandoori Fish

1 pomfret, cleaned
2½ tsps ground chilli
1 tsp garam masala
250 ml yogurt
1 tsp cumin seeds, ground
1 clove garlic, ground
Juice of a small lemon
Salt to taste.

### METHOD

1. Blend yogurt, chilli powder and cumin powder.
2. Clean, dry the fish and make vertical slits on either side of the fish.
3. Rub fish with a mixture of lemon juice, garlic and salt.
4. Marinate the fish in the yogurt mixture. Leave covered for 25 – 30 minutes.
5. Then grill in a medium oven.
6. When it is cooked on one side, turn over on the other side. When ready sprinkle garam masala and serve hot. Garnish with onion rings and lemon wedges.

# West Indies Baked Prawn Curry in Coconut

30 large prawns, shelled
5 egg yolks
300 ml coconut milk, thick
1½ tsps curry powder for fish
¼ tsp cardamom powder
2 small onions, minced
Salt to taste
Oil

### METHOD

1. Beat egg yolks, coconut milk and salt together.
2. Heat oil, saute onions and then add curry powder, stirring until brown.
3. Add in prawns and when partially cooked, remove.
4. Combine the coconut mixture with the cooked ingredients and pour into cleaned empty coconut shells or shell.
5. Bake in a medium oven for 30 – 40 minutes, sprinkle with cardamom powder and serve hot.

# Balinese Prawns in Coconut (Indian Style)

575 g prawns, shelled
1 whole coconut, cleaned
4 cm stick cinnamon, crushed
a few coriander leaves
50 g coconut, ground
7 dried chillies, ground
5 peppercorns, ground
4 cloves, ground
3 cardamom pods, ground
2 large onions, ground
½ tsp cumin seeds, ground
1 tsp ground ginger
1 tsp ground turmeric
40 g ghee
Salt to taste
Flour

### METHOD

1. Rub prawns with the ground ingredients and salt, allowing to stand for 10 – 15 minutes.
2. Clean and cut the top of a large coconut, scoop out flesh. Fill with prawn mixture and crushed cinnamon.
3. Seal the coconut top with the paste made from the flour, then bake for 30 minutes or until done.
4. Remove the contents of the coconut (the cooked prawn mixture) and allow to cool.
5. Heat ghee, fry the coriander leaves for a minute then add the prawn mixture and scramble it for a few minutes over a medium heat. Serve.

*Balinese Prawns in Coconut.*

# Malay Curried Prawns

350 g king-sized prawns, unshelled but cut whiskers off
375 ml coconut milk, thick
75 g pineapple, cut into small cubes
12 small onions, ground
1 tsp shrimp paste, ground
¼ tsp ground turmeric
3 red chillies, ground
5 slices galangal, ground
2 stalks lemon grass, crushed
½ tsp sugar
Salt to taste
Oil

### METHOD

1. Heat two tablespoons oil, fry ground ingredients for 2 – 3 minutes.
2. Then add coconut milk, salt, sugar and lemon grass and bring to a boil.
3. Add pineapple and cook gently until it bubbles.
4. Add prawns, simmer uncovered until prawns are just cooked.

# Indonesian Skewered Prawn (Sate)

35 king prawns, shelled, de-veined
120 g peanuts, fried, ground coarsely
60 ml coconut milk
1 stalk lemon grass, ground
1 tbsp lemon juice
1 clove garlic, mashed
1 tsp chilli powder
½ tsp shrimp paste
1½ tbsps peanut oil
Salt to taste

### METHOD

1. Combine lemon grass, peanuts, chilli powder, lemon juice, coconut milk and salt.
2. Fry shrimp paste and garlic in moderately hot oil for 5 minutes.
3. Add in the combined ingredients, stir together until well blended, and remove.
4. Thread de-veined prawns on skewers, coat on one side with the paste and grill.
5. Then turn them over, spread on the remaining paste and grill until cooked.

# Indian Prawn Kebab

40 king sized prawns, shelled
50 small onions, peeled, halved
15 red chillies, de-seeded
4 tbsp ghee
1½ tsps garam masala
1 tsp turmeric powder
1 tsp ground ginger
1 small onion, ground
Pinch of cumin seeds, ground
Salt to taste

### METHOD

1. Thread prawns on skewers, alternating with onions and chillies.
2. Fry the following ingredients in moderately hot oil: garam masala, ground ingredients, turmeric powder and salt for 3 – 4 minutes, stirring briskly.
3. Coat on one side with the fried paste and grill until brown and cooked.
4. Then turn them over, spread on the remaining paste and grill.

# Chinese Chillied Shrimps

255 g fresh shrimps, shelled, de-veined, drained
2 tbsps minced ginger
2 cloves garlic, crushed
1 tbsp tomato ketchup
1 tbsp chilli sauce
¼ tsp pepper, crushed
¼ tsp chilli powder
1 tbsp dry sherry
1 tbsp soya sauce
2 tbsps peanut oil
1 tsp sugar
3 tbsps spring onions, chopped
Salt to taste
Oil

### METHOD

1. Deep fry the shrimps in heated oil until brown, drain.
2. Remove excess oil, leaving two tablespoons.
3. Add spring onion, garlic and ginger. Stir for about 2 minutes. Discard garlic.
4. Add shrimps and stir fry for another minute; then add dry sherry, soya sauce, sugar and salt to taste. Stir for a while.
5. Then add the chilli sauce, tomato ketchup, pepper and chilli powder. Mix again and remove.

# Indian Prawns in Yogurt

40 large prawns, shelled
30 g ghee
280 ml yogurt
1 sprig curry leaves
2 tsps curry powder
2 peppercorns, crushed
1 clove garlic, crushed
3 red chillies, pounded
2 small onions, sliced
Salt to taste

## METHOD

1. Fry onions in moderately hot oil until soft, then add in the pounded chillies, curry leaves and garlic.
2. Turn the heat to low and allow to cook for 5 minutes or until mixture changes colour, then add curry powder.
3. Stir for a further 4 minutes, add in prawns, pepper, yogurt and salt and bring to boil. Lower the heat, stirring and allowing to simmer until cooked.

# Anglo-Asian Prawn Curry

225 g large prawns, shelled
250 ml coconut milk, thick
60 g butter
1 tsp curry powder
1 tbsp flour
½ tsp pepper
Salt to taste

## METHOD

1. Stir in curry powder in melted butter over a low heat.
2. Gradually add flour, pepper and salt.
3. When the ingredients change colour, add milk.
4. When the gravy begins to thicken, add prawns and simmer until cooked.

# Poultry

*I want there to be no peasant in my realm so poor*
*that he will not have a chicken in his pot every Sunday.*
> — Henry IV, France

# Basic Chicken Curry

3 chicken breasts, cleaned
4 large tomatoes, chopped
2 large onions, sliced
1 tsp ground ginger
100 ml water
2 tbsps oil
1 tsp curry powder for meat
2 cloves garlic, crushed
½ tsp salt

## METHOD

1. Mix the ground ginger and garlic with the chicken and allow to stand for 1 hour.
2. Heat oil, fry onions to a light colour.
3. Now add the curry powder, stir until it begins to ␣␣␣ colour.
   ␣␣␣ and fry for 4 minutes.
   ␣␣␣ tomatoes and salt and after 3 minutes, add ␣␣␣ simmer covered on a low heat until ␣␣␣ is tender and gravy is thick.

# icken Curry For Beginners

2 chicken breasts
2 cloves garlic, crushed
½ tsp curry powder for meat
250 ml coconut milk, thick
2 small onions, sliced
1 green chilli, sliced
½ tsp ground ginger
Salt to taste

## METHOD

1. Mix well the ingredients together with the chicken and cook uncovered over a low fire until chicken is tender.

# Indian Chicken Curry

1½ kg chicken disjointed
450 ml water
4 tbsps butter
2 tbsps sesame seeds, pounded
150 g large onions, sliced thinly
2 cloves garlic, sliced
¼ tsp ginger powder
2 tsps coriander seeds, pounded
1 tsp cumin seeds, pounded
½ tsp chilli powder
1 tbsp turmeric powder
2 tsps salt
1 tsp garam masala

## METHOD

1. Combine all the pounded and powdered ingredients with salt.
2. Rub this mixture into the chicken.
3. Melt the butter, brown onions and garlic. Then add chicken.
4. Add water. Cover and cook over a low heat until chicken is tender. Remove cover for the last 10 minutes and before covering the pot again sprinkle garam masala.

# Pakistani Stewed Chicken

455 g chicken, jointed
250 ml curd
125 ml water
125 ghee
6 medium-sized potatoes, quartered
6 medium-sized tomatoes, chopped
1 large onion, sliced
3 green chillies, sliced
10 almonds, blanched, ground
7 peppercorns, freshly ground
1 tsp garam masala
¼ tsp turmeric powder
Salt to taste

## METHOD

1. Brown onions in heated ghee, then add chicken and ground ingredients.
2. Fry over a medium heat for 3 minutes, then add curd, water, chillies, potatoes, tomatoes, turmeric powder and salt. Cover the pot and simmer for 45 minutes until liquid has nearly evaporated.
3. Sprinkle garam masala and cover the pot. Serve after 2 minutes.

# Indian Chicken Korma (1)

670 g chicken, chopped
  2 cloves garlic, crushed
 20 small onions, sliced
  3 cloves
  4 cardamom pods
  5 cm stick cinnamon
175 ml coconut milk, thick
550 ml coconut milk, thin
  1 sprig curry leaves
  2 tbsps coriander seeds, ground
  1 tbsp cumin seeds, ground
  2 tsps fennel seeds, ground
  2 tsps black peppercorns, ground
  1 tsp turmeric powder
  4 tbsps ghee
  1 tbsp ground ginger
Juice of ½ lemon
Salt to taste

---

METHOD

1. Heat ghee. Fry garlic, ginger, curry leaves and onions until brown.
2. Add cloves, cardamom pods, cinnamon, turmeric powder and ground spices. Fry for 2 minutes.
3. Add the chicken and salt. Fry until well mixed and then add thin coconut milk. Lower the heat and cook uncovered until chicken is tender.
4. Add thick coconut milk and lemon juice. Stir and then cover the pot until the gravy has reached the consistency to your taste.

# Indian Chicken Korma (2)

  6 chicken pieces
  4 small onions, chopped
  2 cloves garlic, crushed
500 ml yogurt
Coriander leaves or mint
  1 tsp grated fresh ginger
  1 tsp turmeric powder
  ½ tsp ground cumin
  2 tbsps ghee
Pepper and salt to taste

---

METHOD

1. Combine yogurt, 2 small onions, garlic, salt and pepper for marinade.
2. Place the chicken in the marinade for 12 hours.
3. Cook in a skillet over a medium heat until most of the yogurt has evaporated.

4. Saute the remaining onions, then add ginger, turmeric powder, cumin powder and stir for 2 minutes.
5. Spoon this mixture into the skillet and continue to cook until it sticks to the pan. Sprinkle garam masala and coriander leaves, cover. Remove skillet after a minute.

# Sri Lanka Chicken Korma

  1 kg chicken, chopped into cubes
250 ml yogurt
  5 cm stick cinnamon
 15 cashew nuts, ground
 10 small onions, sliced
  3 green chillies, ground
 40 g ground coconut
1½ tsps lime juice
  4 tbsps ghee
  3 cardamom pods
  3 cloves
  2 tsp coriander seeds, ground
1½ tsps chilli powder
  1 tsp ground ginger
  3 cloves garlic, ground
  1 sprig curry leaves
Pinch of fragrant spice powder (see page 7)
Salt to taste

---

METHOD

1. Combine ground coconut, garlic, ginger, green chillies, coriander and cashew-nuts.
2. Add meat to this mixture and allow to marinate for 45 minutes.
3. Heat ghee. Fry onions, cardamom pods, cinnamon, cloves, curry powder, chilli powder, curry leaves with the meat. Add salt to taste and cook uncovered on a low heat until chicken is tender and the gravy is thick. Add lime juice.
4. Sprinkle fragrant spice powder, cover for 2 minutes and then serve.

# Indian Tandoori Chicken

1¼ kg chicken
200 ml yogurt
  2 cardamom pods, crushed
  2 large onions, ground
  2 cloves garlic, ground
  1 tsp chilli powder
  ½ tsp coriander, ground
  1 tsp ground ginger
1½ tbsps ghee
  1 tbsp lime juice
  1 tsp garam masala
Salt to taste

GARNISH
  3 medium-sized tomatoes
lettuce
  1 small lemon, wedged
  1 large onion
  ½ tsp garam masala
  1 tsp lemon juice

---

METHOD

1. Combine yogurt with garlic, onions, ginger, coriander, chilli powder, cardamom and garam masala.
2. Skin chicken except on the wings, and quarter it.
3. Make tiny slits in several places in the flesh. Rub with lemon juice and salt as it makes it easier for the marinating sauce to penetrate during the marinating process.
4. Place the chicken in a large shallow baking dish and cover with the marinade. Leave it for 24 hours, turning it over several times.
5. When ready to cook arrange the chicken on a broiler rack and brush with the marinade and ghee. It can be grilled over medium hot charcoal. It can also be transfered onto a baking tray and cooked for 1½ hours over a medium heat at 175 C.
6. Serve chicken on lettuce. Sprinkle garam masala and lemon juice. Garnish with lemon wedges, sliced tomatoes and onion rings.

Note:
To produce an authentic tandoori chicken, the bird must be 340 g in weight and the secret lies in the preparation process. It imparts a special flavour if it has been cooked in a clay oven.

*Indian Tandoori Chicken.*

# Indian Chicken Vindaloo

1 kg chicken
4 small onions, sliced
3 cloves garlic, chopped
3 red chillies, sliced
125 ml vinegar
400 ml hot water
½ tbsp vindaloo paste
¼ tsp turmeric powder
1 tsp garam masala
5 tbsps ghee
¼ tsp ginger, minced
Salt to taste

## METHOD

1. Grind 2 onions, garlic, turmeric, ginger, chillies with vinegar.
2. Mix well the ground ingredients with the chicken and allow to marinate for 2 hours.
3. Heat ghee, fry 2 onions until brown; then add vindaloo paste and stir very gently over a medium heat for 4 minutes.
4. Add chicken with its marinade, salt, water and bring to a boil, then allow to simmer until the gravy thickens.
5. Sprinkle garam masala before removing chicken from the fire.

# Indonesian Chicken in Soya Sauce

1 medium sized chicken, chopped
2 small onions, ground
1 tbsp dark soya sauce
1 tsp brown sugar
1 tomato, peeled, chopped
1½ tsps white vinegar
3 fresh red chillies, ground
2 cloves garlic, ground
3 slices galangal, ground
3 candlenuts, ground
Salt to taste
Oil

## METHOD

1. Rub chicken pieces with vinegar and salt; then deep fry until brown. Remove.
2. Heat a tablespoon oil, fry the ground ingredients until fragrant.
3. Add water, sugar, soya sauce and tomato. Cook the chicken in this sauce until the gravy is quite thick and the chicken is tender.

# Indonesian Barbecued Chicken

1 chicken, cleaned
4 cloves garlic, minced
5 dried chillies
1 large onion, minced
1 tsp shrimp paste, roasted
1½ tsps black pepper powder
Juice of small lemon
Salt to taste
Oil

## METHOD

1. Pound onion, garlic, chillies, shrimp paste, salt and add a little water to form a paste.
2. Rub chicken with oil, pepper and salt.
3. Then barbecue it, basting regularly with the paste until chicken is tender and very brown.
4. Serve with Indonesian peanut sauce (see page 20).

# Indonesian White Chicken Curry

1 medium sized chicken, chopped
250 ml coconut milk, thick
3 cloves, ground
12 peppercorns, ground
2 small onions, sliced
4 candlenuts, ground
1 stalk lemon grass, sliced
2 tsps coriander seeds, ground
½ tsp cumin seeds, ground
¼ tsp galangal powder
¼ tsp fennel seeds, ground
2 cm slice fresh ginger, ground
5 cm stick cinnamon, ground
Juice of ½ lemon
Salt to taste
Peanut Oil

## METHOD

1. Combine all the ground ingredients together.
2. Heat a tablespoon oil, saute onions until soft.
3. Add spice paste. Stir for two minutes, add chicken pieces and stir for another minute or two until chicken is well coated.
4. Add lemon grass, galangal powder and a little water.
5. When the chicken is partially cooked, add coconut milk. Cover and simmer until chicken is cooked and tender.
6. Finally add lemon juice and salt, stir and serve.

# Singaporean Chicken with Satay Flavour

455 g chicken, diced
250 ml coconut milk, thick
250 ml coconut milk, thin
3 large onions, sliced
1 sprig curry leaves
2 stalks lemon grass, pounded
7 g shrimp paste, pounded
7 red chillies, pounded
8 dried chillies, pounded
15 small onions, pounded
5 candlenuts, pounded
1 tsp fresh minced turmeric, pounded
2 tbsps minced galangal, pounded
Salt to taste
Oil

### METHOD

1. Pound all the pounded ingredients together, adding salt and then mixing with the chicken pieces.
2. Heat four tablespoons oil. Fry curry leaves and sliced onions. Remove.
3. Add chicken mixture and fry for a while, adding another tablespoon of oil until oil rises to the surface.
4. Add thin coconut milk, cover and simmer over a low heat until liquid has nearly all evaporated.
5. Add thick coconut milk, fried curry leaves and onions. Cook until the mixture is well blended and the gravy has reached a consistency to your taste.

# Malaysian Chicken Curry

1 chicken, jointed fairly large
500 ml coconut milk, thin
180 ml coconut milk, thick
10 ml tamarind water
6 cloves, ground
6 fresh chillies, ground
7 cloves garlic, ground
5 candlenuts, ground
1 tsp turmeric powder
2 tsps poppy seeds, ground
2 tsps cumin seeds, ground
1 tbsp coriander seeds, ground
20 white peppercorns, ground
7 dried chillies, ground
10 small onions, ground
10 g shrimp paste, roasted, ground
2 stalks lemon grass, ground
Salt to taste
Oil

### METHOD

1. Heat oil. Fry all ground ingredients and turmeric powder until fragrant.
2. Add chicken pieces, stir for 5 minutes, then add thin coconut milk, tamarind water and salt. Cover and simmer until cooked.
3. Add thick coconut milk and salt. Cook and stir briskly for 5 minutes, remove.

# Malaysian Spiced Chicken Fricasse

1¼ kg chicken, chopped into pieces
250 ml coconut milk, thick
20 small onions, minced
2 cloves garlic, minced
1 large onion, sliced
4 tbsps oil
5 tbsps grated coconut
2 tbsps coriander seeds, ground
1 tsp anise, ground
½ tsp cumin seeds, ground
1 tsp freshly ground pepper
1 tsp cinnamon, ground
1 cardamom, ground
2 cloves, ground
¼ tsp nutmeg
Pepper and salt to taste

### METHOD

1. Combine coriander, anise, cloves, cinnamon, cardamom, nutmeg, cumin, pepper and salt.
2. Cut the chicken into pieces, wash, dry and prick with a fork.
3. Combine the spice mixture with the chicken pieces and let it stand for 1 hour.
4. Heat the oil, fry the grated coconut, spiced, chicken, minced onions, garlic and sliced onion and stir for 3 minutes.
5. Add coconut milk, cover and simmer over a low heat until chicken is tender. There should be very little gravy.

# Malay Barbecued Chicken

225 g chicken meat
  8 small onions, pounded
  2 cloves garlic, pounded
  2 tsps brown sugar
  2 tbsps peanut oil
  2 tsps castor sugar
  1 tsp coriander seeds, ground
½ tsp cumin seeds, ground
½ tsp turmeric, ground
½ tsp chilli paste
  1 tsp salt
100 ml tamarind water
Coconut oil for basting
  1 large cucumber, sliced
  2 large onions, wedged

---

METHOD

1. Cut the meat into 2.5 cm slices squarely.
2. Combine ground and pounded ingredients into a paste.
3. Heat peanut oil, fry the paste for 2 – 3 minutes.
4. Add tamarind water, castor and brown sugars, salt and simmer for another 3 minutes.
5. Remove and allow to cool, then add meat and allow to marinade for 12 hours.
6. Thread the meat on skewers and grill over a charcoal fire, basting with peanut oil till cooked.
7. Serve with satay sauce (see page 20) and sliced cucumber and onion wedges.

# Indonesian Spicy Chicken Livers

450 g chicken livers, diced
125 ml coconut milk, thick
  3 cloves garlic, ground
  4 cm lemon grass, bruised, sliced
10 dried chillies, ground
  1 tsp shrimp paste, roasted
  1 tsp galangal powder
  1 tsp brown sugar
  4 small onions, ground
Juice of ¼ small lemon
Pinch of salt
Oil

---

METHOD

1. Combine onions, garlic, shrimp paste and chillies and pound them to a fine paste.
2. Heat 2 tablespoons oil. Fry combined ingredients until they are aromatic and brown.
3. Add liver and fry until it changes colour.
4. Add galangal powder, lemon grass, lemon juice, sugar, salt and coconut milk.
5. Cook uncovered until the oil comes to the surface.

*Indonesian Spicy Chicken Livers.*

# Chinese Spicy Chicken Livers

450 g chicken livers
1 tbsp sugar
1 tsp star anise powder
2 slices fresh ginger
2 tbsps dry sherry
3 tbsps soya sauce
¼ tsp chilli powder
60 ml water

## METHOD

1. Combine ginger, sherry, soya sauce, sugar, anise, chilli powder with the liver and bring to the boil.
2. Stir for a minute or two, then add water. Turn the heat to medium, cover and cook for 10 minutes. Cool. Cut or slice the livers and serve.

# Braised Chicken in Spices

1¼ kg young chicken, jointed
250 ml water
1 stalk lemon grass, chopped
5 coriander roots, chopped
6 cloves garlic, chopped
5 small onions, chopped
7 dried chillies, minced
2 peppercorns
1 tsp shrimp paste
1 tsp galangal powder
½ tsp ground cinnamon
1 tsp tamarind pulp
2 tbsps fish sauce
6 tbsps oil
Salt to taste

## METHOD

1. Grind the following ingredients: lemon grass, coriander roots, garlic, onions, chillies, peppercorns, shrimp paste, galangal powder, cinnamon and salt to taste.
2. Heat oil, fry the ground ingredients until fragrant.
3. Add chicken pieces and stir until they are well coated.
4. Turn the heat to high, add the water and bring to a boil.
5. Cover, reduce heat to low and continue to boil the mixture, stirring occasionally, until the chicken is tender.
6. Add tamarind pulp dissolved in two tablespoons water and fish sauce. Cook for another 3 minutes.

# Hungarian Paprika Chicken

1 kg chicken, chopped
3 large tomatoes, peeled, chopped
2 green capsicums, sliced
1 tbsp flour
1 tbsp paprika
1 tsp pepper
350 ml chicken broth
100 ml milk
2 large onions, sliced
2 cloves garlic, crushed
4 tbsps lard
Salt to taste

## METHOD

1. Heat lard. Fry onions and garlic until tender. Then mix paprika and stir for a minute.
2. Add chicken pieces and cook until brown.
3. Add pepper, salt and chicken broth. Simmer covered for 25 minutes.
4. Add tomatoes, green capsicums and cook until chicken is tender.
5. Mix flour with the milk and stir into the chicken mixture. When it is heated through, remove.

# Lebanese Fried Chicken

225 g chicken, minced
1 large potato, cubed
2 eggs, beaten
few coriander leaves
1 large onion, minced
1 tsp pepper
¼ tsp curry powder for meat
Salt to taste
Oil

## METHOD

1. Heat 3 tablespoons oil, fry onion until brown.
2. Add chicken, pepper, curry powder and salt, stirring for 10 minutes on a low heat.
3. Add potato and when it is nearly cooked, add coriander leaves. If more oil is required to fry the potato, add a tablespoon or two.
4. Add eggs and scramble into mixture and when set, remove.

# Pakistani Duck Korma

1 kg duck, quartered
10 small tomatoes, chopped
200 ml yogurt
120 g ghee
15 almonds, blanched, ground
2 tbsps coriander seeds, ground
7 peppercorns, freshly ground
3 cardamom pods, ground
10 small onions, sliced
3 green chillies, sliced
Salt to taste

### METHOD

1. Combine cardamom, pepper, coriander, almond with yogurt and marinate the duck for 4 hours.
2. Fry onions and chillies until soft; then add duck pieces and fry for 3 – 4 minutes. Add all the ingredients and simmer covered on a low heat until duck is tender.

# Curried Turkey

1¼ kg turkey meat, small pieces
1 large onion, sliced
3 cardamom pods
5 cloves
2 sticks cinnamon, each 3 cm long
4 tomatoes, chopped
7½ tbsps ghee
500 ml water
1 sprig curry leaves
4 cloves garlic, ground
3 tbsps coriander seeds, ground
1¼ tsps chilli powder
1 tsp turmeric powder
1¼ tsps ground ginger
1 tbsp minced onion
1½ tbsps tomato puree
3 tbsps yogurt
Salt to taste

### METHOD

1. Combine turkey with ground spices, minced onion, yogurt, turmeric and chilli powder, tomatoes and salt. Leave it aside for 10 minutes.
2. Heat ghee. Fry cardamom pods, cinnamon, cloves, sliced onion and curry leaves until fragrant.
3. Add turkey meat, fry about 4 minutes over medium heat. Then add water, cover and bring to a boil.
4. When curry is boiling, lower the heat. Add tomato puree, simmer until turkey is tender.

# Singaporean Steamed Roast Duck

1 kg duck
4 slices fresh ginger
1½ tsps star anise powder
1 tsp white peppercorns, ground
1 tsp clove, ground
2 stalks spring onions, chopped
Salt and pepper to taste
Oil

### METHOD

1. Combine ginger, star anise, white pepper, clove and spring onions together.
2. Clean duck. Rub with pepper and salt inside and outside thoroughly.
3. Stuff the combined ingredients inside the duck and steam till tender. Then discard the spices from the duck.
4. Deep fry the duck until brown, turning when necessary. Serve with Singaporean sauce (see page 19) and tomato wedges.

# Turkey Curry

1 kg turkey, medium sized pieces
4 small potatoes, halved
1 sprig curry leaves
475 ml water
100 ml coconut milk, thick
3 tbsps curry powder for meat
½ tsp freshly ground pepper
6 tbsps ghee
1 tsp garam masala
Salt to taste

### METHOD

1. Combine turkey with curry powder, pepper, salt and coconut milk and then leave to marinate for about 15 minutes.
2. Heat ghee. Fry curry leaves, then add turkey and marinade and stir-fry till fragrant.
3. Add water and potatoes. Cover pan and boil, stirring now and then.
4. When potatoes are half cooked, reduce the heat and let curry simmer over a low heat. Remove when the gravy becomes a little thick. Sprinkle garam masala, cover for a while before serving.

# Sri Lankan Rabbit Curry

700 g rabbit meat, chopped into small pieces
15 small onions, halved
2 cloves garlic, crushed
1 sprig curry leaves
1 green chilli, sliced
4½ tbsps ghee
250 ml water
½ tsp mustard seeds
1 tsp fragrant spice powder (see page 7)
1 tsp minced ginger
10 dried chillies, roasted, ground
2½ tbsps coriander seeds, roasted, ground
½ tsp cumin seeds, roasted, ground
½ tsp fennel seeds, roasted, ground
10 black peppercorns, roasted, ground
Salt to taste

METHOD

1. Combine rabbit meat with ginger, garlic, chilli, ground spices, salt and leave it to marinate for 15 minutes.
2. Heat ghee, fry onions, mustard seeds and curry leaves for a minute. Add rabbit, stirring till fragrant. Add water, simmer covered, stirring once or twice during cooking.
3. When the gravy is thick, sprinkle fragrant spice powder. Remove.

# Indian Pigeon Curry

1 kg pigeon, cleaned, quartered and cut into pieces
4 small onions, grated
¼ tsp grated ginger
7 tbsps oil
250 ml water
3 tbsps coriander seeds, roasted, ground
½ tsp cumin seeds, roasted, ground
½ tsp turmeric powder
1 tbsp yogurt
7 dried chillies, roasted, ground
Salt to taste

METHOD

1. Combine pigeon with ground ingredients, turmeric powder, yogurt, ginger, salt and a little water.
2. Heat ghee, add pigeon pieces, fry till fragrant, then add onion. Stir-fry for a while, then add water, cover, and simmer over a low heat until pigeon is tender and the gravy is thickened.
3. Sprinkle garam masala before removing pigeon from the fire.

# Cambodian Chicken Curry

750 g chicken, quartered
1 litre coconut milk
55 g roasted peanuts, skinned
7 small potatoes, peeled, halved
100 ml coconut milk, thick
1 tbsp butter
2 tbsps curry powder for meat
1¼ tsps chilli powder
3 cloves garlic, minced
5 small onions, chopped
Salt to taste

METHOD

1. Brown onion and garlic in heated butter until soft.
2. Stir in the spices and salt and mix well.
3. Bring the heat to low, add 1 litre coconut milk, chicken pieces and potatoes. Cover and simmer until chicken is cooked.
4. Add thick coconut milk and peanuts and simmer for another 20 minutes.

# Burmese Chicken Curry

1 kg chicken, disjointed
750 ml boiling water
4 small onions, minced
3 cloves garlic, minced
2 bay leaves
5 tbsps oil
2 tsps curry powder, S.E. Asian blend
½ tsp chilli powder
1 tsp cinnamon powder
2 tbsps light soya sauce
¼ tsp turmeric powder
Salt to taste

METHOD

1. Wash, dry chicken; then rub with a mixture of soya sauce, curry powder and turmeric powder.
2. Saute onions and garlic in heated oil until brown.
3. Add chicken and brown lightly.
4. Add water, cinnamon powder, chilli powder, bay leaves and salt. Cover and cook over a low heat for 40 – 45 minutes or until chicken is tender. Discard leaves.

# Thai Chicken with Chestnuts

455 g chicken meat, deboned, chopped into pieces
125 g chestnuts, shelled, boiled, halved
400 ml chicken stock
   4 chicken livers, diced
   1 tbsp jaggery (palm sugar)
   4 cloves garlic, chopped, ground
   2 tbsps oil
1½ tbsps coriander roots, pounded
   1 tsp peppercorns, ground
Salt to taste

METHOD

1. Combine garlic, coriander roots and peppercorns into a paste.
2. Heat oil, fry the paste, stirring for a couple of minutes.
3. Add chicken pieces and stir-fry until they are just light brown.
4. Pour in the chicken stock and simmer for 4 minutes.
5. Stir in the chestnuts, chicken livers, salt and palm sugar. Cover and cook for 5 – 7 minutes until chicken is tender.

# Vietnamese Chicken Curry

1¼ kg chicken breasts
750 ml water
   3 large potatoes, peeled, quartered
   1 tbsp curry powder, S.E. Asian blend
   6 tbsps oil
   2 cloves garlic, crushed
   2 small onions, crushed
   2 red chillies, ground
¼ tsp pepper
Salt to taste

METHOD

1. Rub chicken with garlic, onions, pepper and salt; let it stand for 1 hour.
2. Then heat four tablespoons oil, fry chicken until brown.
3. Then add curry powder. Stir, add water and bring to a boil.
4. Reduce the heat and simmer until chicken is tender.
5. Heat the remaining oil, fry potatoes until brown, add chilli paste, stir for a minute or two; then add chicken with the gravy and simmer for 10 minutes or until all the ingredients are well mixed.

*Thai Chicken with Chestnuts.*

*Tahitian Chicken with Pineapple.*

# Tahitian Chicken with Pineapple

   1 kg chicken, disjointed
200 kg pineapple, cubed
   4 large tomatoes, chopped
   2 small onions, crushed
300 ml coconut milk, thick
   1 tsp fresh ginger, grated
   1 tsp curry powder, S.E. Asian blend
   2 cloves garlic, crushed
 ½ tsp pepper
Salt to taste
Oil

## METHOD

1. Season chicken with pepper and salt; then brown on all sides in moderately hot oil over a medium heat. Remove.
2. Combine onion, garlic, ginger, tomatoes and curry powder blended with coconut milk.
3. Pour this mixture over the chicken and bake uncovered until chicken is tender.
4. Add pineapple cubes and cook 5 minutes longer

# Fijian Chicken Curry

   5 chicken breasts
   1 fresh small raw mango
   4 tbsps butter
250 ml coconut milk, thick
1½ tbsps curry powder
 ½ tsp chilli powder
 ¼ tsp ground ginger
Salt to taste

## METHOD

1. Peel, stone and slice mango.
2. Fry chicken in moderately heated butter until brown on both sides.
3. Add curry powder, chilli powder, ginger and salt, stirring for 3 minutes until cooked.
4. Add coconut milk and mango and allow to simmer covered until gravy is thick.

## Samoan Coconut and Spinach Chicken Curry

1¼ kg. chicken
425 g spinach, cleaned, chopped
2 tbsps oil
350 ml coconut milk
4 tbsps butter
½ tsp curry powder, S.E.Asian blend
Salt to taste

METHOD

1. Debone and cut chicken into small cubes. Then brown in heated oil.
2. Add coconut milk, curry powder and salt. Cover and cook over a low heat for 25 minutes.
3. While the chicken is cooking, melt the butter in a saucepan; add spinach and salt to taste.
4. Cover and cook over a low heat for 15 minutes.
5. Now add the chicken with the remaining coconut milk gravy; bring to a boil and serve.

## West Indian Chicken with Peanuts

1 kg. chicken, jointed
500 ml chicken stock
75 g roasted peanuts, ground
2 small onions, minced
2 cloves garlic, minced
1 tsp coriander seeds, ground
½ tsp ground ginger
1 tsp garlic, ground
West Indian peanut butter* or ghee
Salt to taste

METHOD

1. Saute onions, garlic lightly; then add chicken pieces and fry until brown.
2. Remove excess West Indian peanut butter leaving a tablespoon, then add chicken stock, ground garlic, ginger, coriander, ground peanuts and salt to taste.
3. Simmer uncovered until chicken is tender and gravy is thick.

*Note:
This is not the peanut butter used as a sandwich spread.

## Indian Grilled Duck

1 small duck, cleaned, halved
1 tbsp ginger, ground
250 ml yogurt
3 cloves garlic, ground
2 small onions, ground
Pepper and salt to taste

METHOD

1. Combine ginger, garlic, onion, pepper, salt with yogurt.
2. Marinate the duck pieces for 12 hours and grill, basting regularly with its marinade.

## Thai Fried Chicken

3 chicken breasts, cleaned, dried
1½ tsps peppercorns, ground
2 cloves garlic, ground
1 tbsp coriander roots, ground
Oil for frying

METHOD

1. Rub the ground paste all over the chicken breasts. Allow to stand for at least 30 minutes.
2. Deep fry in heated oil until brown and tender. Drain on paper towels and serve with Thai Dressing for salads (see page 22).

# Meat

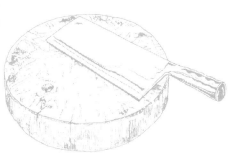

*"That is your poem — too tenuous for a book,*
*You are a very gentle perfect cook."*

— *Walter Lowenfels*

# Basic Meat Curry

225 g lamb meat
250 ml water
  1 tomato, chopped
  2 green chillies, sliced
  3 tbsps butter
  1 large onion, sliced
2½ tsps curry powder for meat
  1 tsp chilli powder (optional)
Salt to taste

### METHOD

1. Cut the lamb meat into small cubes.
2. Combine with tomato, curry powder, chillies, chilli powder, onion and salt.
3. Heat butter on a medium heat; fry lamb pieces until brown.
4. Add water, cover pot and bring to a boil, then simmer, stirring now and then. When the meat is tender and gravy becomes fairly thick, remove.

# Curried Meat

225 g meat
100 g tender peas
125 ml milk, undiluted
200 ml water
2½ tsps curry powder for meat
  1 large onion, sliced
  1 green chilli, sliced
Salt to taste

### METHOD

1. Cut meat into small pieces.
2. Combine it with onion, chilli, curry powder, water and salt. Bring to a boil, stirring all the time, then lower the heat and simmer covered until meat is tender.
3. Add milk and peas and cook until peas are soft.

# New Zealand Lamb Chops

 4 lamb chops
 2 medium sized tomatoes, sliced
Butter
½ tsp garam masala
 2 cloves garlic, ground
 1 tsp ground ginger
½ tsp curry powder for meat
Salt to taste

### METHOD

1. Rub the chops with the mixture of garlic, ginger and salt.
2. Saute in heated butter over a medium heat until brown on both sides.
3. Sprinkle with curry powder, then add sliced tomatoes and bake in a medium oven for 5 minutes. Dab on butter. Bake again for 3 minutes.
4. Sprinkle garam masala before removing from the oven.

Note:
For garnish see page 34.

# Indian Lamb Chops

400 g lamb chops (6 pieces)
200 ml water
  7 tbsps ghee
  6 peppercorns, ground
  1 tsp cumin seeds, ground coarsely
  1 tbsp coriander seeds, ground
  2 tsps chilli powder
  1 tsp turmeric powder
Salt to taste

### METHOD

1. Combine the following ingredients: cumin, coriander, chilli powder, turmeric, pepper and salt to taste with a little water to form a paste. Then rub it over lamb chops.
2. Heat ghee, fry chops until browned.
3. Add water, cover and simmer over a low heat until meat is tender and almost dry.

Note:
For garnish see page 34

# Indonesian Lamb Chops

450 g lamb chops (7 pieces)
250 ml stock
  4 red chillies, ground
  2 small onions, crushed
  5 peppercorns, ground
  2 laurel leaves, crushed
½ tsp nutmeg
  1 tsp ground ginger
1½ tbsps lemon juice
  2 tbsps soya sauce (Javanese)
Peanut oil
Salt to taste

### METHOD

1. Heat two tablespoons oil, fry ground and crushed ingredients until fragrant.
2. Add lemon juice, salt, stir well and then add chops, stirring until the chops are well coated with ingredients.
3. Add nutmeg, soya sauce, laurel leaves and stock.
4. Allow to simmer on low heat until chops are dry and tender.

Note:
For garnish see page 34

# Pakistani Mutton Curry

225 g mutton, chopped
250 ml curd
  2 green chillis, sliced
  2 cloves garlic, crushed
  5 cm stick cinnamon, crushed
  2 tomatoes, halved
½ tsp coriander powder
½ tsp cumin powder
¼ tsp turmeric powder
  6 peppercorns, ground
  1 large onion, sliced
Ghee
Salt to taste

### METHOD

1. Fry onions in moderately heated ghee until brown.
2. Add peppercorns and powdered ingredients, cinnamon, and stir for a while.
3. Gradually add curd, salt, chillies, garlic and tomatoes.
4. Place mutton on top of the ingredients, close the pot tightly, cook over a medium heat until meat is cooked.

# Indonesian Mutton Curry

455 g mutton, 4 cm pieces
600 ml coconut milk
  50 g roasted coconut, ground
  10 dried chillies, ground
  10 black peppercorns, ground
   4 cloves garlic, ground
   4 cm lemon grass, ground
   1 tsp fennel seeds, ground
   1 tsp cumin seeds, ground
   1 tsp ground ginger
   2 cardamom pods, ground
¼ tsp nutmeg, grated
   1 tsp turmeric powder
   2 cm stick cinnamon
Juice of ½ small lemon
Oil
Salt to taste

### METHOD

1. Heat four tablespoons oil, fry onions, garlic, cinnamon, nutmeg and cardamom for two or three minutes over a medium heat.
2. Add ground spices with the ground roasted coconut and lemon grass, stirring for a while.
3. Add meat and stir until the meat is well coated with the spices.
4. Add coconut milk, turmeric powder and salt, simmer covered until meat is tender.
5. Add lemon juice before removing pot from the fire.

# Sri Lankan Pork Curry

455 g pork, chopped
400 ml water
  2 cloves garlic, chopped
  4 cm lemon grass, chopped
  1 sprig curry leaves
  1 tsp cumin seeds, ground
  1 tsp fennel seeds, ground
  2 tsps coriander seeds, ground
2¼ tsp chilli powder
 ½ tsp pepper
Salt to taste

## METHOD

1. Roast the following ingredients: cumin, coriander, chilli powder, fennel, pepper, garlic, lemon grass, and curry leaves to a brown colour.
2. Combine roasted ingredients with meat, water and salt.
3. Bring to a boil, then simmer over a low heat until meat is tender.

# Singaporean Pork Curry

300 g pork, chopped
500 ml coconut milk, thin
 75 ml coconut milk, thick
 10 small onions, pounded
  1 sprig curry leaves
  4 candlenuts, pounded
  5 fresh chillies, pounded
  5 dried chillies, pounded
1¼ tsps shrimp paste, pounded
  1 tbsp galangal, pounded
1½ tbsps curry powders for meat
Salt to taste
Oil

## METHOD

1. Heat three tablespoons oil, fry pounded ingredients until the mixture becomes fragrant.
2. Add curry powder and continue to stir well over a medium heat.
3. Add pork and fry for another 4 minutes.
4. Add thin coconut milk and curry leaves. Bring to a boil, then simmer and cook gently till the pork is tender.
5. Add thick coconut milk and salt. When gravy has thickened to taste, remove.

# Thai Pork Stuffed in Oranges

455 g ground pork
112 g chopped skinned peanuts
  3 cloves garlic, minced
  2 tbsps oil
  7 large Thai oranges
 ½ tsp coriander seeds, ground
 ½ tsp chilli powder
  2 tsps fish sauce
  1 tsp shrimp powder
Salt to taste

## METHOD

1. Saute the garlic, then add the pork, peanuts, coriander, chilli, fish sauce, shrimp powder and salt. Cook over a low heat, stirring frequently, until meat is cooked.
2. Cut the unpeeled oranges halfway down in four sections, leaving the skin connected at the bottom. Remove the pith, flatten and stuff with the pork mixture.
3. Arrange in a baking pan. Bake over a medium heat for 10 minutes.

# Indonesian Braised Pork

455 g pork, cut into 1 cm pieces
 15 small onions, minced
  3 cloves garlic, minced
 60 ml Javanese soya sauce
  1 tsp chilli powder
  1 tsp lemon juice
  2 tsps brown sugar
  3 tbsps oil

## METHOD

1. Saute the pork in heated oil; add onions and garlic. Stir in the chilli powder.
2. Add soya sauce, sugar, and lemon juice. Cook over low heat for 10 minutes or until cooked.

# Indian Minced Meat Curry

250 g minced meat
100 g tender peas
  1 large potato, peeled cut into 1 cm cubes
  1 large onion, cut into 1 cm cubes
  2 cloves garlic, ground
  2 cm piece ginger, ground
  1 large red capsicum, cut into ½ cm strips
  1 medium-sized tomato, cut into 2 cm slices
½ tsp cumin seeds, ground
  2 tbsps curry powder
  1 tsp garam masala
  6 tbsps oil
Salt to taste

### METHOD

1. Combine minced meat with ginger and garlic paste, curry powder, cumin, salt and a little water.
2. Heat oil, fry the capsicum and then remove.
3. In the same oil, fry onion and stir until brown. Then add meat and fry till fragrant.
4. Add potato, stir, then add 250 ml water and bring to a boil.
5. Cover and continue to cook until potato is soft.
6. Add tomato, peas and cover and cook for 5 minutes. Then add capsicum and sprinkle with garam masala.

# African Lamb Stew

375 g lean lamb
125 g peanuts, roasted, ground
675 ml water
  2 cloves garlic, ground
  5 large tomatoes, chopped
  4 small onions, chopped
10 red chillies, crushed
½ tsp curry powder for meat
Salt to taste
Oil

### METHOD

1. Chop lamb into small pieces.
2. Brown lamb in heated oil, then add onions, curry powder, tomatoes and water. Allow to stew for half an hour.
3. Blend peanuts with a little water and add to the lamb mixture.
4. Stir, then add chillies, garlic and salt. Allow to bubble for a few minutes over a low heat, then remove.

# Indian Lamb Curry

425 g lean lamb
250 ml yogurt
200 g ghee
125 ml water
  50 g tomato puree
  2 large onions, sliced
  1 tsp cumin seeds, ground
  2 tsps chilli powder
½ tsp freshly ground pepper
  1 tsp ground ginger
  3 cloves garlic, ground
Salt to taste

### METHOD

1. Cut meat into 2 cm pieces, then add salt and yogurt. Cover and leave in pot for 12 hours.
2. Fry onions in heated ghee until brown, then add ginger, garlic and water. Simmer for 10 minutes.
3. Add cumin, chilli, pepper and simmer for another 7 minutes.
4. Add tomato puree, stir for 4 minutes then add meat with the marinade and cook gently for 1 – 1¼ hours or until meat is tender.

# Indian Lamb Korma

455 g lean lamb
300 ml yogurt
  2 cloves garlic, crushed
  1 large onion, chopped
  2 cardamom pods, crushed
  2 tbsps butter or ghee
  1 tsp coriander powder
½ tsp cinnamon powder
  1 tsp ground ginger
1½ tsps turmeric powder
Pepper and salt to taste
Pinch of garam masala

### METHOD

1. Cut the meat into 2.5 cm pieces and rub with ginger and salt.
2. Combine yogurt with cinnamon, coriander, cardamom and add the meat and marinate for 10 – 12 hours.
3. Saute the onion and garlic in the butter or ghee until tender.
4. Stir in the turmeric and cook for a minute, then add the meat and marinade. Cook covered on low heat for about 1 – 1¼ hours or until meat is tender. Sprinkle a little garam masala.

# Indian Curried Meatballs

225 g minced meat
125 g roughly grated onions
100 g onions coarsely chopped
 30 g breadcrumbs
 60 g butter
  1 egg yolk
125 ml yogurt
 70 ml meat stock
 ½ tsp chilli powder
 ½ tsp ground pepper
 ½ tsp turmeric powder
 ½ tsp cumin seeds
  1 tsp minced ginger
  1 tsp garam masala
  2 cloves garlic, minced
Oil for frying
Salt to taste

---

METHOD

1.  Mix the meat with the grated onions, garlic, egg yolk, cumin seeds, breadcrumbs and seasoning.
2.  Form into walnut-sized balls; deep fry in oil until cooked.
3.  Fry chopped onions in butter in another pan until brown.
4.  Add ginger, salt and spices and stir in the stock.
5.  Simmer 10 – 15 minutes then add meat balls and yogurt. Bring to a boil, then simmer until it begins to bubble.
6.  Sprinkle garam masala.

Note:
For garnish see page 34

*Indian Curried Meatballs.*

# Indian Mutton Curry

455 g mutton, chopped
225 g potatoes, quartered
125 ml vinegar
500 ml coconut milk, thick
   6 large onions, chopped
   6 cloves garlic, chopped
   5 green chillies, sliced
   2 tbsps coriander powder
   1 tbsp chilli powder
   1 tsp cumin powder
   1 tsp ground ginger
   1 tsp turmeric powder
   1 tsp mustard seeds
   1 tsp curry powder
   2 tsps ground rice flour
Salt to taste
Ghee

---

### METHOD

1. To moderately hot ghee, add onions, garlic, chillies, mustard seeds, curry powder, coriander powder, chilli powder, cumin powder, turmeric powder and ginger. Stir constantly, then decrease heat.
2. Add mutton and fry it, then add coconut milk and vinegar.
3. Simmer on very low heat until meat is nearly tender, then add potatoes.
4. When the potatoes are nearly cooked, add rice flour mixed with a little water and salt. Add more water if necessary.

# Indian Mutton with Lentils and Vegetables

400 g mutton ribs, medium sized pieces
225 g lentils, split yellow grams, soaked overnight
250 ml coconut milk, thick
500 ml coconut milk, thin
600 ml water
   7 small potatoes, peeled, halved
   2 curry bananas, skinned, halved, (cut into 3 cm pieces)
   7 medium sized tomatoes, halved
   2 carrots, skinned, diced
   3 drumsticks, chopped into 3 cm lengths
   3 small eggplants, halved, diced
   1 large onion, sliced
   2 small onions, sliced
   2 sprig curry leaves
   1 clove
   1 tbsp ground ginger
   3 cloves garlic, ground
   2 tbsps curry powder
1½ tbsps tamarind water
   1 tbsp chilli powder
   1 tsp mustard seeds
1½ tsps turmeric powder
   6 tbsps ghee
   1 red chilli, sliced
   3 green chillies, sliced
   5 cm stick cinnamon
   2 cardamom pods
Salt to taste

---

### METHOD

1. Heat ghee, saute large onion, 1 sprig curry leaves, mustard seeds, and chilli powder. When mustard seeds begin to crackle, remove. Reserve.
2. Put mutton ribs, lentils, ground ginger, garlic, turmeric powder, 1 sprig curry leaves, small onions, green chillies, red chilli, cinnamon, cardamom, clove and water in a pot and bring to a boil. Then simmer till lentils are nearly cooked.
3. Add potatoes, drumsticks, carrots, eggplants, bananas, thin coconut milk to curry powder. Cover and bring to a boil for 5 minutes. Then lower the heat and simmer till vegetables are cooked. Add salt. Stir.
4. Add thick coconut milk and tamarind water. Stir, then add tomatoes and the fried ingredients including the ghee. Remove after gravy begins to bubble.

# Indian Mutton with Lentils

500 g mutton
225 g lentils, split yellow grams
225 g small onions, sliced
350 ml water
 60 g ghee
 55 g curd
  9 red chillies, ground
½ tsp turmeric powder
½ tsp cumin seeds, ground coarsely
  5 cloves garlic, crushed
  9 peppercorns, ground coarsely
  1 sprig curry leaves
Salt to taste

---

METHOD

1. Crush 100 g of the sliced onion with cumin and garlic.
2. Combine the following ingredients: crushed ingredients, chilli paste, curd and salt.
3. Cut mutton into 2 cm pieces and marinate it with the curd mixture for an hour. Soak lentils in water for 5 hours.
4. Heat ghee, fry onions and curry leaves, then add meat and cover pan and shake well.
5. Add drained lentils and water and cook over a medium heat.
6. Add pepper and turmeric. Mix well and simmer until almost dry.

# Mexican Minced Meat

225 g minced meat
  1 large carrot, finely sliced
  1 medium sized capsicum, shredded
  1 large onion, finely sliced
  2 tbsps chilli sauce
  2 tsp chilli powder
  2 tbsps oil

---

METHOD

1. Heat oil, add the meat and fry briskly for 10 minutes.
2. Add the chilli sauce and powder, onion, carrot and capsicum and cook for 2 – 3 minutes. Serve with rice.

# Ginger and Pork Casserole

425 g pork, cubed
225 g carrots, skinned, sliced
550 ml water
112 g haricot beans, soaked
  2 red chillies, deseeded, sliced
  1 large onion, chopped
  1 sprig parsley/curry leaves
2¼ tsp ground ginger
1¼ tsps ground cumin
  1 tbsp turmeric powder
  1 tbsp minced fresh ginger
  2 tbsps oil
 2.5 cm stick cinnamon
Salt to taste

---

METHOD

1. Heat oil, fry onion and pork for 10 minutes, stirring occasionally.
2. Add ground ginger, fresh ginger, cumin, turmeric, salt and enough water to cover the meat by 2 cm.
3. Bring to a boil and simmer gently for 25 minutes.
4. Add beans, chilli, carrot, cinnamon and parsley. Cook for a further 20 minutes, until tender.

# Indian Pork Vindaloo

450 g pork, boneless, diced
  1 large onion, sliced
112 g butter
  2 tsps turmeric powder
  1 tsp fenugreek
  2 tsps ginger powder
  2 tbsp coriander powder
  1 tbsp chilli powder
  2 tbsps chilli sauce
  2 tsps mustard powder
  2 tbsps vinegar
  2 tsps ground cumin
Salt/pepper to taste

---

METHOD

1. Blend the spices, sauce and vinegar until smooth.
2. Add the pork, salt and enough water to coat the pork. Stir the marinade well; cover and refrigerate for 12 hours.
3. Fry the onion in butter for 3 minutes, then add the meat and marinade. Bring to a boil and simmer for 45 minutes until the liquid has reduced to a thick, rich sauce.

# Australian Spicy Lamb Liver

350 g lamb liver, chopped
  2 tbsps tomato ketchup
1½ tsps English mustard powder
  1 tbsp oil
  ¼ tsp mild curry powder
  1 tbsp Worcestershire sauce
Salt and pepper to taste

### METHOD

1.  Fry liver in oil for about 10 minutes until cooked.
2.  Stir in tomato ketchup, curry powder, mustard, Worcestershire sauce, pepper and salt.

### Note:

To serve, cover a slice of bread with shredded lettuce leaves and spoon the liver curry over it.

# Indonesian Liver Curry

350 g liver, diced
 10 dried chillies, ground
  6 peppercorns, ground
  2 small onions, ground
  2 cloves garlic, ground
  1 stem lemon grass, ground
  4 candlenuts, ground
2½ tsps coriander seeds, ground
  ½ tsp cumin seeds, ground
  ¼ tsp turmeric, ground
  ½ tsp galangal powder
  1 tsp minced ginger, ground
  1 tsp shrimp paste, roasted, ground
150 ml coconut milk, thick
Salt to taste
Oil

### METHOD

1.  Combine all ground and powdered ingredients.
2.  Heat four tablespoons oil, fry the combined ingredients until brown and aromatic.
3.  Add liver and fry until it changes colour.
4.  Add salt and coconut milk. Cook uncovered until the sauce thickens and oil appears on the surface.

# Iranian Veal Stew

450 g veal, boneless, cut into 1 cm cubes
  2 small onions, chopped
  2 cardamom pods, crushed
200 ml water
  ½ tsp ground coriander
  ½ tsp pepper
  ½ tsp turmeric powder
  2 tbsp oil
Salt to taste

### METHOD

1.  Brown veal cubes in a saucepan.
2.  Add onions, saute, then add coriander, pepper, turmeric, cardamom and salt. Stir for a minute over a medium heat.
3.  Add water and cover. Cook slowly over a low heat until meat is tender.

# Grilled Veal

125 g veal
 50 g sugar
  6 red chillies, ground
Juice of 1 large lemon
  1 large onion, wedged
  1 tomato, wedged
  4 small onions, ground
  4 cloves garlic, ground
  1 tsp coriander powder
  2 tbsps coconut milk or milk
  1 capsicum, wedged
Salt to taste

### METHOD

1.  Combine ground ingredients with lemon juice, coriander powder, coconut milk and salt.
2.  Cut the veal into 2 cm pieces and soak in sugar for 2 hours.
3.  Then rub the meat and wedged ingredients with the combined ingredients. Skewer and grill.

### Note:

Arrange meat, tomato wedges, capsicum wedges, and onion wedges alternately on skewers.

# Indian Lamb with Almonds

1 kg lamb, cut in 1 cm cubes
500 g small onions, chopped
200 g almonds, blanched, ground
6 tbsps ghee
250 ml yogurt
125 ml heavy cream
½ tsp ginger powder
¼ tsp ground cumin
1 tsp freshly ground pepper
1 tbsp turmeric powder
1 sprig curry leaves
1½ tsps salt

### METHOD

1. Saute onions in three tablespoons ghee until brown. Set aside.
2. Combine the following ingredients: ginger, turmeric, cumin and lamb.
3. Melt the remaining ghee and brown lamb in it.
4. Add onions, curry leaves, yogurt and salt. Cover and cook over low heat until meat is tender.
5. Blend ground almonds with the cream and add to lamb mixture. Simmer for 10 minutes. Taste for seasoning.

# Malay Tamarind Meat

325 g stewing meat, cut into small pieces
500 ml water
3 tomatoes, chopped
3 tbsps oil
250 ml tamarind water
26 dried chillies, soaked, ground
3 red chillies, ground
5 cm lemon grass, bruised
sugar/salt to taste

### METHOD

1. Heat oil. Fry chilli paste and meat for 20 minutes.
2. Add tamarind water and cook over a medium heat, stirring well.
3. Add tomatoes, water and lemon grass and bring to a boil.
4. Lower the heat. Cover the pan and simmer, stirring occasionally until the meat is tender. Then add sugar and salt. The gravy should be of a thick consistency.

*Indian Lamb with Almonds.*

*Thai Pork and Prawns.*

# Burmese Pork Meatballs

450 g pork, ground
125 g raw prawns, shelled, chopped
    3 eggs, beaten
    4 tbsps oil
Pinch of chilli powder
    ½ tsp pepper
    2 cloves garlic, minced
    2 small onions, minced
    2 tsps lemon juice
Salt to taste

### METHOD

1.  Mix all the ingredients except oil.
2.  Shape into flat croquettes; then heat oil and fry them lightly.
3.  Add croquettes to 150 ml boiling water. Cover and cook over low heat for 30 minutes.

**Note:**
For garnish see page 34

# Thai Pork and Prawns

225 g prawns, shelled, minced
225 g minced pork
250 ml coconut milk, thin
    2 red chillies, minced
    ½ tsp pepper
    1 tsp sugar
    1 tsp ground chilli
Salt to taste

### METHOD

1.  Combine pork and prawn together.
2.  Heat coconut milk over a low heat and when it simmers, add combined mixture. Stir well and bring to a boil.
3.  Reduce heat, uncover. Add pepper, salt, sugar, ground chilli and minced chillies. Stir for a while and when it is heated through, remove.

# Indian Meat Vindaloo

   1 kg meat (cross rib or chunk), cut into 4 cm pieces
125 ml vinegar
200 g small onions, ground
   3 cloves garlic, minced, ground
   2 tsps ground coriander
   2 tsps turmeric powder
   1 tsp ground ginger
   1 tsp cumin powder
   5 tbsps butter
   2 tsps salt

METHOD

1. Grind the following ingredients together adding vinegar gradually: coriander, turmeric, ginger, cumin, garlic, onions and salt until almost a paste.
2. Combine with the meat and marinate for 24 hours. Chill.
3. Melt the butter or ghee. Add the undrained meat and stir. Then add the marinade. Cover and cook over a low heat for 1½ hours, stirring frequently until meat is done.
4. Add a tablespoon of water if necessary.

# Singaporean Meat Stew

450 g stewing meat, chopped
500 ml coconut milk
  75 g grated coconut, roasted, ground
  13 small onions, pounded
   8 red chillies, pounded
   1 stalk lemon grass, pounded
   2 tbsps minced galangal, pounded
   1 tsp sugar
  ½ tsp turmeric powder
  ½ tsp monosodium glutamate
   5 tbsps oil
   1 tsp salt

METHOD

1. Heat oil, fry pounded ingredients and turmeric powder for 2 minutes.
2. Add meat pieces, stirring until the meat becomes brown.
3. Then add salt, sugar, monosodium glutamate, coconut milk and roasted coconut. Cover and simmer over a low heat, stirring now and then until meat is tender and dry.

# British Meat Curry

450 g meat fillet, cut into 2.5 cm pieces
350 ml meat stock
   1 small apple, minced
   2 small onions, minced
   3 small potatoes, halved
  30 g butter
   1 tbsp ground almond
  ½ tbsp curry powder for meat
   1 tsp lemon juice
Salt to taste

METHOD

1. Heat butter. Fry meat lightly on both sides and remove.
2. Fry the onions lightly and add curry powder. C ok slowly for 15 minutes, then add almond (mixed with a tablespoon of water), stock, apple, lemon juice and salt. Bring to a boil.
3. Add meat and potatoes and simmer uncovered till tender. Serve with rice.

# Malay Mutton Curry

450 g mutton, chopped
   7 small onions, pounded
   7 red chillies, pounded
   5 dried chillies, pounded
250 ml coconut milk, thick
500 ml coconut milk, thin
   2 tbsps curry powder (S.E. Asian blend)
   1 tsp shrimp paste, pounded
   4 cm lemon grass, bruised
   4 small potatoes, quartered
Salt to taste
Oil

METHOD

1. Heat three tablespoons oil. Fry pounded ingredients with curry powder until fragrant.
2. Add meat and salt and fry until meat is well coated and brown.
3. Add thin coconut milk and lemon grass, lower the heat and simmer uncovered until meat is nearly tender.
4. Add potatoes and cook till soft.
5. Then add thick coconut milk and cook for 2 – 3 minutes. Remove.

# Indian Dry Mutton Curry

450 g mutton, chopped
  9 small onions, sliced
  5 cm stick cinnamon
  2 cardamom pods
  3 cloves
250 ml water
  2 tbsps curry powder
  2 tsps chilli powder
½ tsp ground ginger
½ tsp ground garlic
  1 sprig curry leaves
Juice of lime
Salt to taste
Ghee

---

### METHOD

1. Mix the ground and powdered ingredients with a little water to form a paste.
2. Rub the meat with the paste.
3. Heat three tablespoon ghee. Fry cinnamon, cardamom pods, cloves, onions and curry leaves, keep aside. In the same pan, add meat and fry till oil rises to the surface.
4. Now add the fried ingredients, water and salt. Cover and bring to a boil. Then lower the heat, simmer until meat is cooked. (Do not open the lid during this part of cooking till fragrance emits from the pot.)
5. Sprinkle lime juice over it. Serve.

# Vegetables
# & Lentils

*We eat food for its texture,*
*as well as for fragrance, flavour and colour.*
*— Asian wisdom*

# Basic Vegetable Curry

450 g French beans
  30 g butter
   6 tbsps cream or top of milk
   1 tbsp lemon juice
  ½ tsp mild curry powder
Pepper and salt to taste

### METHOD

1. Cook sliced beans in boiling salted water. Drain.
2. Heat butter with lemon juice, cream and curry powder.
3. Toss in the beans, simmer for 2 minutes or until it is heated through. Sprinkle in a pinch of pepper and salt to taste.

# Basic Vegetable Curry (2)

  4 small potatoes, boiled, quartered
  1 small onion, sliced
  4 tbsps coconut milk
Pinch of garam masala
  2 tsps butter
½ tsp curry powder
Salt to taste

### METHOD

1. Heat butter and fry the onions to a pale gold colour.
2. Add curry powder and the potatoes. Mix well and fry for 5 minutes over a low heat.
3. Add coconut milk and salt, stir and cook uncovered till potatoes are dry. Sprinkle a pinch of garam masala before removing from the fire.

# Ladies' Fingers in Tomato Sauce

225 g ladies' fingers, chopped
225 g canned tomatoes
  1 large onion, chopped
  1 green chilli, deseeded, minced
  2 cloves garlic, crushed
  1 tsp coriander seeds, coarsely ground
¼ tsp turmeric powder
  1 tsp chopped mint
  2 tbsps oil
  2 tbsps butter

### METHOD

1. Fry ladies' fingers and garlic in blended butter and oil for 5 minutes or until brown.
2. Add onion, chilli, coriander seeds, turmeric powder, mint and tomatoes. Simmer, covered for 20 minutes.

# Indian Cabbage Curry

450 g cooked shredded cabbage
  1 large onion, sliced
  3 green chillies, sliced
  2 red chillies, sliced
100 g ghee
  1 tsp ground ginger
½ tsp turmeric powder
  1 tsp garam masala
  1 tsp mustard seeds
  1 sprig curry leaves
  1 clove garlic, sliced
Salt to taste

### METHOD

1. Fry onion, garlic, green and red chillies, curry leaves and mustard seeds in heated ghee until the mustard seeds begin to crackle.
2. Now add the cabbage with the turmeric, garam masala, ground ginger and salt. Stir on a medium heat until the cabbage is well heated through and becomes very dry.

# Malay Cabbage Curry

450 g cabbage, shredded
250 ml coconut milk
  10 small onions, sliced
   3 cloves garlic, sliced
   1 tsp shrimp paste, roasted
   1 tsp chilli powder
  ½ tsp turmeric powder
Salt to taste

### METHOD

1. Combine the coconut milk, shrimp paste, chilli powder, turmeric powder, garlic, onions and salt and bring to a boil.
2. Now add cabbage. Cover and cook over low heat for 30 minutes.

# Thai Fried Bean Sprouts

225 g bean sprouts, cleaned, drained
200 g pork, cut into 1 cm x 5 cm strips
150 g prawns, shelled
  4 cloves garlic, crushed
  ½ tsp pepper
  1 tsp sugar
  1 tbsp fish sauce
  3 tbsps oil
  1 tsp shrimp powder

METHOD

1. Heat oil, fry garlic until brown.
2. Then add pork and stir-fry a minute. Add prawns.
3. Sprinkle with shrimp powder, fish sauce, sugar and pepper.
4. Stir in the bean sprouts and mix with the other ingredients and cook over a medium heat for 3 minutes.

# Indonesian Spinach Curry

225 g spinach, chopped
125 ml coconut milk, thick
  2 cloves garlic, pounded
  2 small onions, sliced, pounded
  ½ tsp chilli powder
1½ tsps shrimp paste, roasted, pounded
  3 tbsps oil
Salt to taste

METHOD

1. Heat milk and boil spinach. Set aside.
2. Combine all the pounded ingredients with chilli powder and salt. Pound.
3. Heat oil. Fry combined ingredients until fragrant, then add coconut milk and cooked spinach. Stir, and when well mixed and heated through, remove.

# Singaporean Fried Water Convolvulus

85 g water convolvulus, chopped
  2 dried chillies, broken into pieces
  1 small onion, minced
½ tsp chilli powder
¼ tsp curry powder
Salt to taste
Oil

METHOD

1. Fry onion, chillies, until fragrant.
2. Add spinach and stir for a while.
3. Add salt, chilli powder and curry powder, stirring well until cooked.

# Sri Lankan Jaffna Spinach

75 g spinach, cleaned, chopped
  3 small onions, sliced
  2 cloves garlic, sliced
  1 tsp coconut, ground
  3 green chillies, sliced
Salt and lime juice to taste

METHOD

1. Combine onions, chillies, garlic with spinach and simmer on a low heat for about 5 minutes.
2. Add coconut and salt. Stir and cook for another 3 minutes. Mash. Add lime juice to taste before serving.

# Burmese Fried Spinach

225 g spinach, cleaned
  1 clove garlic, sliced
  1 small onion, sliced
  1 tbsp oil
¼ tsp chilli powder
¼ tsp turmeric powder
½ tsp fish sauce
  1 tbsp water
Salt to taste

METHOD

1. Drain the cleaned spinach, shred coarsely.
2. Heat oil, fry onion, garlic, chilli powder, fish sauce, turmeric powder and salt for 3 minutes over a medium heat.
3. Add spinach and water. Cover and cook over a low heat until cooked.

# American Cauliflower with Cheese and Curry Sauce

 1 large cauliflower, cut into florets
250 ml milk
 1 small can tomatoes
 90 g cheese, grated
 30 g butter
 1 tbsp flour
 1 tsp mild curry powder
Pepper/salt to taste

METHOD

1. Boil the cauliflower in salted water, drain and keep hot.
2. Melt the butter, stir in the flour and cook for 2 – 3 minutes.
3. Blend in the milk gradually and bring to the boil.
4. Add the tomatoes, cheese, curry powder and seasoning. Reheat but do not boil. Pour over the cauliflower; sprinkle with pepper.

# British Cauliflower Curry

 1 large cauliflower
250 ml curry sauce for cauliflower (see page 18)
Parsley

METHOD

1. Boil the cauliflower in florets in salted water, drain and keep hot.
2. Pour the hot curry sauce over the cauliflower; sprinkle with parsley.

# British Turnips with Cheese and Curry

 3 turnips
90 g butter
60 g grated cheese
 3 tbsps stock
½ tsp mild curry powder
Salt and pepper to taste

METHOD

1. Cook turnips in boiling salted water until tender. Drain.
2. Mash well with 30 g butter and stock. Season well.
3. Put into a greased fireproof dish, sprinkle cheese and curry powder on top and add remaining butter. Bake in a hot oven for 15 minutes until the top is golden.

# Hawaiian Baked Eggplant

 1 large eggplant peeled and sliced thinly
225 ml coconut milk, thick
 30 g butter
15 small onions, sliced thinly
 ½ tsp curry powder
 ½ tsp chilli powder
 1 tbsp chopped coriander leaves
Salt to taste

METHOD

1. Arrange eggplant in a buttered dish.
2. Sprinkle with onions, curry powder, chilli powder, coconut milk and salt.
3. Cover with a sprinkling of coriander leaves and bake until eggplant is tender.

*American Cauliflower with Cheese and Curry Sauce.*

# Sri Lankan Cucumber Curry

1 large cucumber, skinned
120 ml coconut milk, thick
7 small onions, sliced
3 green chillies, sliced
1 tbsp Maldive fish powder
¼ tsp tamarind water
Pinch of turmeric powder
Curry leaves
Salt to taste

METHOD
1. Remove core from cucumber and cut into rounds.
2. Put all the ingredients together and simmer over a low fire until cooked.

# Pakistani Potato Curry

7 small potatoes, peeled, sliced
4 cloves garlic, ground
3 small onions, ground
85 g ghee
120 ml curd
1 tsp chilli powder
½ tsp ground ginger
½ tsp cumin seeds, ground
9 peppercorns, freshly ground
2 cardamom pods, ground
1 clove, ground
Salt to taste

METHOD
1. Blend ground spices with the curd.
2. Heat ghee, fry potatoes until nearly brown. Add salt and chilli powder, st r.
3. When well mixed, add curd mixture. Cover and allow to simmer until cooked and dry.

# Indian Potato Curry

450 g potatoes, peeled, quartered
250 ml water
3 tbsps ghee
2 tsps coriander powder
½ tsp chilli powder
1 tsp turmeric powder
Salt to taste

METHOD
1. Melt the ghee, stir in the turmeric and then add potatoes.
2. Saute until nicely browned. Then add coriander powder, chilli powder, salt and water. Cover and cook until potatoes are tender.

Note:
This curry is particularly good with Indian bread.

# Indian Potato Mash

3 large potatoes, boiled, mashed coarsely
1 large onion, minced
1 red chilli, minced
A few curry leaves
4 green chillies, minced
1 tsp minced ginger
100 ml yogurt
3 tbsps coconut milk, thick
Salt to taste

METHOD
1. Combine all the ingredients together.
2. Bring to the boil. Remove and serve.

# Pakistani Pumpkin Curry

350 g pumpkin, sliced
125 ml curd
90 g minced lamb
90 g ghee
10 small onions, sliced
1 tsp mixed spices (see page 6)
½ tsp mild curry powder
½ tsp ground ginger
1 tbsp ground coriander
3 cloves garlic, crushed
7 peppercorns, freshly ground
Salt to taste

METHOD
1. Combine curry powder, ground ginger, ground coriander and pepper.
2. Heat ghee, fry onion lightly; then add mixed spices and garlic. Stir for a while.
3. Add meat and when it is quite cooked, add pumpkin, curd and salt. Simmer on low heat for 20 minutes until all ingredients are cooked and dry.

# Indian Pumpkin Curry

450 g pumpkin, cubed
8 dried chillies, fried
1 large onion, sliced, fried
5 cloves garlic, fried
225 g coconut, grated, fried
200 g prawns, shelled (optional)
1 tsp ghee
½tsp mustard seeds
1 tsp fenugreek seeds, fried
1 tbsp coriander seeds, fried
1 tsp minced turmeric, ground
1 tbsp tamarind water
Salt to taste
Water

METHOD

1.  Grind all the fried ingredients together with turmeric and tamarind water.
2.  Boil pumpkin and prawns in sufficient water. Add salt to taste.
3.  When cooked, add ground ingredients and simmer.
4.  Heat ghee, add mustard seeds and curry leaves. When mustard seeds start to splutter add mixture to the pumpkin curry. Stir, and when it comes to a boil, remove.

# Pakistani Turnip Curry

450 g turnip, boiled, peeled, sliced
75 g ghee
10 small onions, sliced
9 peppercorns, freshly ground
2 cm piece ginger, minced
1 tsp garam masala
½ tsp turmeric powder
½ tsp chilli powder
2 tsps coriander seeds, ground
Salt to taste

METHOD

1.  Heat ghee, fry onions lightly.
2.  Then add turnip, ginger and stir over a medium heat for 5 minutes.
3.  Add spices and salt to taste. Simmer for 5 minutes.
4.  Sprinkle garam masala.

# Indian Pea Curry with Cream Cheese

225 g peas, cooked
225 g Indian cream cheese (panir) (see page vii)
100 g ghee
125 ml water
3 large onions, minced
Coriander leaves
½ tsp chilli powder
½ tsp ground ginger
½ tsp garam masala
Salt to taste

METHOD

1.  Cut the panir or Indian cream cheese into 1 cm cubes; then fry in heated ghee until brown on both sides. Remove, drain.
2.  Now add the onions and fry until golden brown.
3.  Add panir cubes, peas, ginger, chilli powder, salt water and stir very gently for 2 minutes.
4.  Add garam masala and coriander leaves, stir for a minute, remove. Serve at once.

# Indian Vegetables with Yogurt

350 g green peas, cooked
2 large tomatoes, peeled, chopped
4 medium sized potatoes
2 small onions, chopped
1 clove garlic, crushed
500 ml yogurt
1 sprig curry leaves
1 tsp chilli powder
1½ tsps turmeric powder
½ tsp coriander seeds, ground
4 tbsps ghee oil
½ tsp cumin seeds, ground
Pepper and salt to taste

METHOD

1.  Wash, cook potatoes in boiling salted water. Drain, peel, cube.
2.  Heat oil, fry onion and garlic until tender.
3.  Add turmeric, cumin, coriander and chilli powders. Season with salt and pepper.
4.  Stir for a minute. Add potatoes and cook until well coated with spices.
5.  Mix in the tomatoes, curry leaves, and peas and cook for a minute.
6.  Add yogurt and when it is heated through, remove.

# Indian Stuffed Eggplants

5 eggplants, round variety
100 g tender peas
100 g carrots, skinned, diced
225 g tomatoes, peeled, chopped
100 g ghee
1 tsp white pepper, ground
1 tsp minced ginger
1 tsp curry powder for vegetable
1 large onion, chopped
Salt to taste

---

METHOD

1. Cut the eggplants into halves, scoop out the pulp leaving 1 cm around. Boil pulp in slightly salted water till partially cooked. Drain.
2. In a frying pan, fry onions until brown. Then add peas, carrots, and chopped pulp. Fry for 3 minutes then add tomatoes. Simmer until vegetables are nearly cooked.
3. Add salt, ginger, curry powder, stir for 2 minutes. Sprinkle pepper.
4. Arrange the eggplant halves in a baking tray and fill each half with the fried pulp. Bake it in an oven at 175°C until brown.

# Indian Yam Curry

450 g yams, peeled, cut into 2 cm cubes
2 small onions, sliced
3 green chillies, sliced
100 g ghee
1½ tsps coriander powder
½ tsp ginger juice
½ tsp garam masala
½ tsp chilli powder
Salt to taste

---

METHOD

1. Fry yam cubes in ghee and drain.
2. Fry onions lightly then add garam masala, chilli powder, coriander powder, green chillies, ginger juice and salt. Stir for a minute; then add yam.
3. Cover and simmer over a medium heat until yam is dry and well mixed in spices.

*Indian Stuffed Eggplants.*

# Indian Vegetables Cutlets

450 g potatoes, boiled, mashed
150 g tender peas, crushed
  3 green chillies, minced
  1 small onion, minced
  2 small onion, minced
  2 tbsps minced coriander leaves
225 g semolina or breadcrumbs
  ½ tsp turmeric powder
  ½ tsp cumin seeds
  2 tbsps coconut, grated
2½ tbsps cornflour
Ghee
Salt to taste

### METHOD

1. Heat two tablespoons of ghee. Fry onion, peas, chillies, turmeric, salt, coriander, cumin seeds and coconut for 4 minutes.
2. Add cornflour to mashed potatoes and knead well. Divide and roll into lemon-sized balls.
3. Flatten each ball, fill with a spoonful of vegetable mixture, roll again, press to flatten, and coat with semolina or breadcrumbs.
4. Deep fry until golden brown and serve with tomato sauce.

# Indian Fried Vegetable Curry

  3 eggplants, cut into bite sized pieces
  5 potatoes, cut into bite sized pieces
100 g young peas
225 ml water
  4 tbsps oil
  1 tsp mustard seeds
  1 tsp chilli powder
  1 tsp black gram
  1 tsp turmeric powder
  ¼ tsp asafoetida
Salt to taste

### METHOD

1. Prepare a total of 400 g of vegetables.
2. Heat oil, add mustard seeds, asafoetida and black gram.
3. When mustard seeds begin to crackle, add vegetables, chilli powder, turmeric powder, water and salt. Cook until vegetables are tender.
4. Sprinkle a little water over the vegetables to aid softening and to prevent sticking to the pan.

# Indonesian Fried Vegetable Curry

225 g french beans
225 g ladies' fingers
300 g prawns, shelled
  6 tbsps water
  7 dried chillies, ground
  ¼ tsp galangal powder
  1 tbsp shrimp paste
  4 tbsps oil
  4 candlenuts, ground
  1 small onion, minced
Salt to taste

### METHOD

1. Pound shrimp paste, onion, chillies, candlenuts and galangal powder into a fine paste. Cut vegetables into small rounds.
2. Fry pounded paste in heated oil, until an aroma is given out.
3. Add prawns and stir fry for a minute.
4. Add vegetables and later add water and salt. Simmer uncovered until vegetables are cooked.

# Malay Bean Curd Curry

  4 firm bean curd cakes, diced
 20 prawns, shelled
325 ml coconut milk, thick
  1 stalk spring onion, chopped
  3 candlenuts, ground
10 small onions, ground
10 red chillies, ground
  3 dried chillies, ground
  1 tbsp shrimp paste, ground
Salt to taste
Oil

### METHOD

1. Cut the bean curd cakes into 1 cm squares; then fry in heated oil until brown, remove.
2. Remove excess oil, leaving two tablespoons. Fry ground ingredients till fragrant.
3. Add prawns, fry for 2 minutes, add coconut milk and salt.
4. When the gravy begins to bubble, add bean curd, spring onions and cook for 3 minutes over a low fire.

# Indian Mixed Vegetables

      5 potatoes, skinned
      3 eggplants
      3 drumsticks, skinned
      3 yams, skinned
      3 unripe bananas, skinned
      1 large onion, chopped
      3 carrots, skinned
      1 sprig curry leaves
     15 green chillies, ground
      1 raw mango, peeled, chopped
    500 ml curd
    225 g coconut, ground
     75 g runner beans
      1 litre water
      1 tsp cumin seeds, ground
      1 tsp turmeric powder
      2 tsps coriander powder
      5 tbsps raw coconut oil
    Salt to taste

---

METHOD

1. The vegetables should be medium sized and cut into bite sized pieces. Bring the water to a boil in a pot, add vegetables, onion, mango, and turmeric powder. Simmer until the vegetables are tender.
2. Add cumin, coconut, chillies and coriander. Allow to simmer for 10 minutes.
3. Add curd and salt, cook for 4 minutes.
4. Add raw coconut oil and curry leaves. Stir well, remove.

Note:
The delightful aroma of this dish is due to the use of raw coconut oil.

*Indonesian Mixed Vegetables.*

# Indonesian Mixed Vegetables

    105 g cabbage, shredded
    105 g french beans, sliced
    105 g eggplants, sliced
    105 g pumpkin, skinned, sliced
    125 g shelled prawns
    500 ml coconut milk, thick
     60 g grated coconut, roasted
      1 tsp coriander seeds, ground
      2 small onions, ground
      3 cloves garlic, ground
      6 candlenuts, ground
      7 dried chillies, ground
    1½ tsps shrimp paste, roasted, ground
    Salt to taste

METHOD

1. Heat pan. Add curry paste made from ingredients and fry until it is cooked over a low heat.
2. Add coconut milk, eggplants, pumpkin, fresh beans and cabbage; stir.
3. After two minutes add roasted coconut, prawns and salt. Allow to simmer, stirring until all the vegetables are cooked.

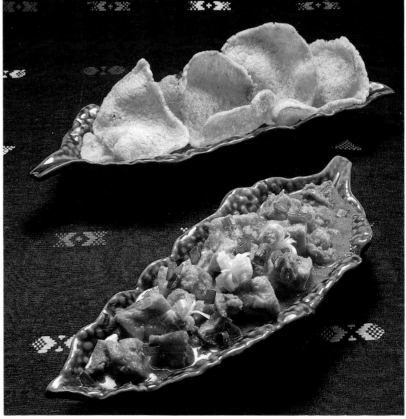

*Malay Bean Curd Curry.*

# Basic Lentil Curry (1)

225 g red split lentils
500 ml water
 ½ tsp turmeric powder
 1 tsp ghee/vegetable oil
Salt to taste

### METHOD

1.  Clean, wash and soak lentils for 4 hours. Drain.
2.  Bring water and lentils to a boil, then add ghee or oil and turmeric powder. Stir, cover and simmer until the lentils are very soft. The consistency should be that of a thick soup.
3.  Add salt. Stir and remove.

# Basic Lentil Curry (2)

225 g yellow split lentils
 1 large onion, chopped
 2 dried chillies, each broken into three bits
 1 sprig curry leaves
500 ml water
250 ml coconut milk, thick
 ½ tbsp curry powder
 ¼ tsp turmeric powder
Ghee
Salt to taste

### METHOD

1.  Clean, wash and soak lentils for 4 hours. Drain.
2.  Cover the lentils with water, add turmeric powder and bring to a boil. Cover, simmer until the lentils are very soft.
3.  Heat two tablespoons ghee. Fry curry leaves, onion, chillies and curry powder and then stir into the cooked lentils.
4.  Simmer for 3 minutes, add salt and coconut milk and simmer again for another 3 minutes. Remove.

# Fried Split Lentils

50 g yellow split lentils, soaked
 1 large onion, sliced
 2 dried chillies, each broken into three bits
Pinch of cumin seeds, crushed
 1 tsp turmeric powder
 1 tsp mustard seeds
 1 sprig curry leaves
Ghee
Salt to taste

### METHOD

1.  Cook lentils in water till very soft. Drain.
2.  Heat two tablespoons of ghee. Fry onion, curry leaves, chillies, mustard seeds, cumin seeds, turmeric powder and salt.
3.  Then add the cooked lentils, mix and cook for 2 minutes. Remove.

# Indian Lentil Curry

225 g red split lentils
500 ml water
 1 small onion, chopped
 1 green chilli, sliced
 2 dried chillies, each broken into three bits
 ½ tsp turmeric powder
 ½ tsp cumin seeds, coarsely ground
 2 tsps ghee
 2 cloves garlic, sliced
Salt to taste

### METHOD

1.  Clean, wash and soak lentils for 4 hours. Drain.
2.  Bring the water and lentils to a boil, then add 1 clove garlic, green chilli, and turmeric powder. Cover, simmer until cooked.
3.  Heat ghee, fry dried chillies, 1 clove garlic, onion and cumin seeds and pour over the cooked lentils. Add salt. Stir for a minute and remove.

# Sri Lankan Jaffna Lentil Curry

225 g red split lentils
500 ml water
30 g coconut, ground
1 sprig curry leaves
10 black peppercorns, freshly crushed
½ tsp turmeric powder
2 green chillies, minced
3 small onions, minced
2 cloves garlic, crushed
Salt to taste

METHOD

1. Clean, wash and soak lentils for 4 hours. Drain.
2. Bring the water, lentils, turmeric powder, chillies, onions, garlic, pepper, curry leaves to a boil. Cover and simmer until lentils are soft.
3. Add coconut and salt and cook for 2 minutes over a medium heat.

# Indian Lentils with Vegetables

125 g lentils, soaked for 12 hours
50 g carrots, skinned, chopped
50 g potatoes, skinned, quartered
50 g peas
3 tomatoes, chopped
500 ml water
250 ml coconut milk, thick
Pinch of turmeric powder
1 tsp garam masala
½ tsp curry powder
1 tbsp ghee
1 large onion, chopped
3 dried chillies, each broken into three bits
1 sprig curry leaves
Salt to taste

METHOD

1. Heat ghee. Fry curry leaves, onion, chillies, curry powder and garam masala. Keep aside.
2. Boil lentils, carrots, potatoes, tomatoes and peas in water for 15 minutes. Cover and simmer until cooked.
3. Add coconut milk, turmeric, salt and the fried ingredients with the cooked lentils and simmer again for 3 minutes.

# Indian Tamarind Lentil Curry

125 g black split lentils
125 g red split lentils
500 ml water
250 ml coconut milk, thick
200 g eggplants, bite-sized pieces
7 dried chillies, each broken into three bits
125 g grated coconut
250 ml tamarind water
1 tsp black peppercorns
1 tsp mustard seeds
1 tsp black split lentils (for frying)
1 tbsp ghee
½ tsp turmeric powder
3 tbsps vegetable oil
¼ tsp asafoetida
Salt to taste

METHOD

1. Put the lentils, water, turmeric and 1 teaspoon of oil into a pot and bring to a boil. Stir. Cover and simmer until the lentils are cooked.
2. In another pan, bring the eggplants with the coconut milk to a boil. Simmer and cook until nearly tender. Add tamarind water and simmer for 5 minutes until the raw smell of the tamarind disappears.
3. Heat 2½ tbsps oil, fry cooked lentils, chillies, peppercorns, salt, asafoetida and coconut gratings to a brown colour. Liquidise or grind the ingredients. Add this mixture to the cooked eggplants.
4. Fry mustard seeds and black lentils in ghee and pour into the lentil and eggplant mixture. Stir well, simmer for 3 minutes, remove.

Note:
If desired, omit tamarind juice, adding instead, 70 ml lime juice.

# Spicy Soups, Broths & Drinks

*Soup of the evening,*
*beautiful soup.*

— *Lewis Caroll*

# Basic Lentil Soup

120 g red lentils
500 ml water
  1 curry leaf/bay leaf
  1 clove garlic, crushed
  1 small onion, chopped
  5 peppercorns, ground
Salt to taste

### METHOD

1. Soak lentils overnight. Drain.
2. Put lentils, water, curry leaf or bay leaf, garlic, onion and pepper in a pot. Bring to a boil. Stir, cover and simmer for 1 – 1½ hours or until the lentils are very soft. Add salt. Stir. Adjust the consistency and seasoning to taste.

### Note:
For garnish see page 35

# Curry Soup

225 g yellow lentils
 15 small onions, chopped
  3 cloves garlic, chopped
  2 tomatoes, chopped
  1 litre water
  1 slice ginger, ground
  1 tbsp curry powder for vegetable
  2 tbsps ghee
Pinch of turmeric powder
Pinch of mustard seeds
Salt to taste

### METHOD

1. Soak lentils in water overnight. Drain.
2. Cook the lentils until it becomes soft.
3. In another pan fry the onions, garlic, tomatoes, ginger, curry powder, turmeric powder and mustard seeds.
4. Pour this mixture into the cooked lentils and add more water if necessary and let it simmer for another 15 minutes. Add salt to taste.

### Note:
For garnish see page 35

# Indian Lentil Soup

120 g lentils
400 ml water
  2 sprigs coriander leaves, chopped
 ½ tsp garlic paste
  2 small onions, sliced
 ¼ tsp chilli powder
 ¼ tsp turmeric powder
 ½ tsp ginger paste
 ½ tsp green chilli paste
Salt to taste

### METHOD

1. Soak lentils in water for 5 hours. Strain. Bring 400 ml water to a boil, then add lentils. Cook until the lentils become soft. Mash.
2. In a pan fry the onions, add the spices and ground ingredients and brown.
3. Pour the cooked lentils into this and add 200 ml water and salt to taste. Simmer for 15 to 20 minutes. Sprinkle coriander leaves.

# British Mulligatawny

400 g neck of mutton
  1 litre stock
  1 carrot, skinned, sliced
  1 turnip, skinned, sliced
  1 apple, chopped
  1 small onion, sliced
  1 tbsp mild curry powder
  2 tbsps flour
  2 tbsps dripping
  1 tbsp lemon juice
Pepper/salt to taste

### METHOD

1. Cut the meat neatly, discarding the bones.
2. Melt the dripping and fry the vegetables, onion and apple lightly. Add curry powder and fry gently for 20 minutes.
3. Then add flour, meat, bones, and stock, mixing well. Season to taste.
4. Bring to a boil, then skim. Simmer slowly for 3 hours, skimming occasionally.
5. Strain the soup and reserve the meat. Reheat and add lemon juice. Serve with meat.

### Note:
For garnish see page 35

# Indian Mulligatawny

500 ml meat stock, rich
30 g butter/ghee
1 small onion, chopped
1 clove garlic, crushed
2 slices fresh ginger, minced
250 ml coconut milk, thick
2 tsps ground coriander
½ tsp turmeric powder
½ ground cumin
½ tsp ground fenugreek seeds
1 lemon, sliced

### METHOD

1.  Melt butter and fry the onions and garlic until softened.
2.  Add ginger, spices and cook for 3 minutes.
3.  Add stock, bring to the boil and simmer for 15 minutes.
4.  Cool slightly then, add the coconut milk with lemon.

# Indian Chicken Mulligatawny

1½ kg chicken, disjointed
2¼ litres water
15 small onions, chopped
2 cloves garlic, ground
1 tsp ground ginger
1 tsp chilli powder
5 peppercorns, whole
2 tsps coriander seeds, ground
1 tsp turmeric powder
1 tsp vinegar
1 tbsp ghee
1 tsp freshly ground pepper (optional)
Salt to taste

### METHOD

1.  Combine chicken, peppercorns, water and salt. Bring to a boil. Cover and simmer until tender. Skim the fat.
2.  Pound the coriander, turmeric and ginger with vinegar.
3.  Melt the ghee and saute the onions lightly. Stir in the chilli powder and fry for a minute or two.
4.  Add garlic, stir for a minute; then add pounded spices and fry until fragrant.
5.  Add to the soup and cook for 15 minutes. Add pepper and salt to taste.
6.  Chicken may be deboned and served in the soup.

# Indonesian Chicken Broth

1 tender chicken
225 g bean sprouts, cleaned, scalded
2 large potatoes, boiled, sliced
120 g shelled prawns
3 small onions, minced
1 tsp turmeric powder
1 tsp minced ginger
¼ tsp shrimp paste
5 cloves garlic, crushed
Salt, pepper and lime juice to taste
Water

### METHOD

1.  Pound prawns, shrimp paste, turmeric powder, salt, ginger, garlic and onions to a fine paste.
2.  Mix these pounded ingredients with chicken and leave it aside for 15 minutes.
3.  Now put the spiced chicken into a pot and add enough water to cover the chicken. Simmer chicken in broth until tender.
4.  Remove the bones, slice the meat and combine with potatoes, and scalded bean sprouts.
5.  Pour the broth over it, and serve with lime juice and pepper.

# Fijian Prawn Head Soup

455 g prawn heads
500 ml coconut milk, thin
125 ml coconut milk, thick
Parsley, chopped
1 tsp curry powder for fish
7 peppercorns, crushed coarsely
Salt to taste

### METHOD

1.  Mix prawn head with curry powder and pepper and leave it to stand for 30 minutes.
2.  Combine it with thin coconut milk and bring to a boil. Simmer uncovered until the liquid has evaporated by half.
3.  Remove and mash prawn heads with the back of a spoon and reheat it again. Add salt.
4.  When the liquid begins to boil, add the thick coconut milk. Stir, then remove and strain into bowls, garnish with parsley.

# Iraqi Lamb Soup

225 g lean lamb
125 g lentils
  2 large tomatoes, chopped
  2 medium sized potatoes, chopped
2¼ litres water
  1 large onion, sliced
  2 cloves garlic, chopped
  5 peppercorns, ground
  ½ tsp turmeric powder
Salt to taste

### METHOD

1. Cut meat into chunks and put in a large pot with lentils, onion, garlic, turmeric powder and 2¼ litres water.
2. Bring to a boil for 10 minutes, then allow to simmer for 2 hours.
3. When the liquid has evaporated by nearly half, add tomatoes, pepper, potatoes and salt. Simmer until the vegetables are cooked.

# Indian Mutton Soup (1)

450 g mutton
  1 green chilli, sliced
  2 cloves
  2 cardamom pods
  5 cm stick cinnamon
  5 small onions, sliced
  1 tomato, chopped
  3 cloves garlic, ground
  2 slices ginger, ground
  2 dried chillies, ground
  3 tbsps coriander powder
1½ tsps black peppercorns, freshly ground
  2 tsps poppy seeds, ground
  1 tsp cumin, ground
  5 tbsps oil
  2 litres water
Salt to taste

### METHOD

1. Cut mutton into small pieces and combine with ground ingredients and powdered ingredients, chilli, and salt.
2. Heat oil. Fry cinnammon, cloves, cardamom pods and onions until onions turn colour.
3. Add meat and fry till fragrant.
4. Add tomato, water and boil till meat is tender. Serve.

# Indian Mutton Soup (2)

250 g mutton (with bones)
  4 tbsps yellow-split lentils
  2 tbsps ghee
  1 tsp coriander powder
  1 tsp turmeric powder
  1 or 2 mint leaves
Coriander leaves
  ½ tsp chilli powder
  ½ tsp garlic paste
  ½ large onion, sliced
  ½ large onion, sliced, fried and ground
Water
Salt to taste

### METHOD

1. Fry till brown the sliced onion. Add chopped mutton, spices and ground ingredients.
2. Add 250 ml water and cook until tender.
3. Cook the lentils in 500 ml boiling water. When soft, mash and add to the meat mixture with 100 ml water. Add salt and simmer. Garnish with a little mint and coriander leaves.

*Indian Mutton Soup.*

# Hawaiian Coconut Milk Soup

700 ml coconut milk
700 ml meat broth
  1 potato, diced
  2 tsps curry powder for vegetable
  2 tbsps cornstarch
Salt and pepper to taste

---

### METHOD

1. Blend the curry powder and cornstarch with a little water, then add mixture to the broth with potato.
2. Simmer uncovered and stir until the soup begins to bubble.
3. Stir in the coconut milk; heat but do not boil.
4. Add pepper and salt to taste.

# Thai Corn and Prawn Soup

225 g cooked shelled prawns
500 g tinned kernel corn or fresh corn
  3 small onions, minced
  4 cloves garlic, crushed
  1 egg, beaten
  1 tbsp oil
  ½ tsp black peppercorns, crushed
1½ tbsps coriander leaves
  2 tbsps fish sauce (nam pla)
750 ml chicken stock
  1 red chilli, thinly sliced

---

### METHOD

1. Fry onion, garlic in heated oil until brown.
2. Add chicken stock, fish sauce, pepper, prawns and corn. Bring to a boil.
3. Add egg and stir into the soup for a minute or two.
4. Pour soup into soup bowls and garnish with coriander leaves and red chilli.

# Burmese Cabbage Soup

700 g cabbage, shredded
225 g onions, chopped
  2 tomatoes, finely chopped
  3 cloves garlic, minced
1½ litres chicken broth
  3 tbsps oil
  1 tbsp shrimp paste
  ½ tbsp tamarind pulp
  1 tsp chilli powder
Salt to taste

### METHOD

1. Blend tamarind pulp, shrimp paste, chilli powder, salt and broth.
2. Heat oil, saute onions and garlic lightly.
3. Add cabbage; saute for 10 minutes, stirring frequently.
4. Now add tomatoes, and blended ingredients and cook over low heat for 30 minutes.

# Indian Pepper Broth — Rasam

250 ml tamarind water
  1 tsp mustard seeds
  1 tbsp rasam powder (see page 4)
  1 litre water
  1 tsp cumin seeds, ground
  1 tbsp gingelly/sesame oil
  1 pinch asafoetida
Salt to taste

---

### METHOD

1. Blend the ground cumin seeds with 1 litre water and tamarind water.
2. Bring to a boil and simmer for 10 minutes.
3. Add the rasam powder, salt and bring to a boil. Add asafoetida.
4. Fry the mustard seeds in oil until it splutters. Pour into the rasam. Remove.

### Note:

Tomatoes can be added to the rasam pepper broth. After adding the rasam powder, the rasam should not be allowed to boil for more than 3 minutes or the flavour will disappear.

# Indian Lime Juice Broth — Rasam

125 g lentils
500 ml water
  1 tsp oil
  1 sprig parsley or coriander, chopped
  5 tbsps lime juice
  1 tbsp gingelly oil
  ½ tsp turmeric powder
  ½ tsp cumin seeds, ground
1½ tsps peppercorns, ground
  ½ tsp chilli powder to taste
  1 tsp mustard seeds
Salt to taste

**METHOD**

1. Bring the water to a boil; then add lentils, turmeric powder and a teaspoon oil. Simmer until the lentils are very soft. Mash.
2. Add ground ingredients, chilli powder, coriander and salt. Add another 250 ml water, stir and bring to a boil. Remove.
3. Add lime juice and mustard seeds fried in 1 tbsp gingelly oil. Stir.

# Indian Thick Gravy — Sambhar

225 g red gram lentil
250 ml tamarind water
  2 tbsps sambhar powder (see page 3)
  1 sprig curry leaves
125 g coconut, ground
  1 litre water
  1 tsp mustard seeds
  1 tsp oil
  ½ tsp fenugreek seeds
Pinch of asafoetida
2 dried chillies, each broken into three bits
Salt to taste

**METHOD**

1. Fry the mustard seeds, curry leaves, fenugreek, chillies and asafoetida in oil till fragrant.
2. Boil the lentils in water until soft. Mash.
3. Then boil the tamarind water with salt until the raw smell of tamarind disappears. Discard tamarind and add lentils to the tamarind liquid.
4. Add sambhar powder, coconut and fried ingredients, stirring well.

**Note:**
A combination of vegetables may be used in a vegetable sambhar.

# Jaffna Coconut Gravy — Sothi

250 ml coconut milk, thick
250 ml water
  5 small onions, chopped
  1 small tomato, chopped (optional)
  ½ tsp turmeric powder
  3 green chillies, sliced
  1 sprig curry leaves
Salt and lime juice to taste

**METHOD**

1. Combine chillies, curry leaves, turmeric powder, onions and water. Bring to a boil, stirring all the time. After 10 minutes, allow to simmer until the gravy has reduced by three-quarters.
2. Mash the ingredients, add coconut milk and salt. Stir for a minute, remove. Add lime juice before serving.

**Note:**
This coconut gravy has the characteristic Jaffna flavour arising from the combination of chillies, onions and curry leaves. You may add fish head or prawn heads in this gravy.

# Indian Curd Gravy

225 g ground coconut
  1 tbsp yellow split lentils
250 ml water
375 ml curd/yogurt
  ½ tsp turmeric powder
  1 tsp fenugreek seeds
  1 sprig curry leaves
  ¼ tsp dry ginger powder
  5 green chillies, ground
  ½ tsp cumin seeds, ground
  1 tsp mustard seeds
  1 tbsp oil
Salt to taste

**METHOD**

1. Grind coconut, lentils, chillies, ginger, cumin, turmeric powder and salt to a fine paste.
2. Mix the ground paste with curd or yogurt and 250 ml water. Bring to a boil. Foam will form on the surface, remove at once.
3. Fry the fenugreek seeds, mustard seeds and curry leaves in oil. When the mustard seeds begin to splutter, pour into the curd gravy.

**Note:**
120 g vegetables can be used. Cauliflower, yam, capsicum, unripe banana and eggplant are boiled and added to this curd gravy. The amount of water should be reduced by half.

# Jaffna Kool

3 tbsp palmyrah root flour
200 g white fish, seared, cleaned
90 g rice
50 g green spinach, chopped
3 cloves garlic, crushed
7 jak seeds, skinned, chopped
10 peppercorns, freshly ground
12 long beans, cut into 3 cm lengths
10 dried chillies, ground
10 small sized crabs, cleaned
60 medium sized prawns, shelled
1 medium sized tapioca, skinned, chopped
3 litres water
250 ml tamarind water (see below)
Salt to taste

METHOD

1. Blend 2 tbsps tamarind concentrate in 250 ml water with ground chillies, palmyrah root flour and pepper.
2. Boil three litres water and add rice. Cook over a medium heat.
3. When it is partially cooked, add chopped tapioca and jak seeds. After 10 minutes, add beans, crabs, fish, prawns and garlic. Simmer uncovered until the ingredients are cooked.
4. Add spinach, salt and blended ingredients and stir continuously until cooked. Adjust seasoning. Pour into serving bowls and serve hot.

*Jaffna Kool.*

*Indian Spiced Buttermilk.*

# Indian Spiced Buttermilk

250 ml yogurt
1½ litres water
　1 sprig curry leaves
　3 tbsps fresh lime juice
　2 green chillies, minced
Salt to taste

---

METHOD

1.　Combine yogurt with water until well homogenised.
2.　Add curry leaves, lime juice, chillies and salt. Chill.

Note:
This drink is very refreshing during hot weather.

# Indian Ginger Tea

750 ml water
　12 raisins
　¼ tsp minced ginger
　1 tsp black peppercorns, whole
　1 tsp cumin seeds
1½ tbsps coriander seeds
Hot milk and sugar to taste

---

METHOD

1.　Bring water with raisins, peppercorns, cumin seeds, coriander seeds and minced ginger to a boil. Boil for 3 minutes, then simmer until it is reduced by two thirds.
2.　Cool and then strain the liquid completely through a thin muslin cloth. Add hot milk and sugar to taste.

Note:
This drink is excellent during cold weather.

# Indian Spiced Sweet Drink

1 litre water
112 g brown sugar
¼ tsp dry ginger powder
¼ tsp cardamom powder

---

METHOD

1. Dissolve the brown sugar in water, stirring well and then strain.
2. Add ginger powder and cardamom powder. Mix well. Chill.

# Sri Lankan Jaffna Lime Drink

2 large lemons
2 small onions, minced
750 ml water
1 green chilli, minced
1 sprig curry leaves
Salt to taste

---

METHOD

1. Squeeze the juice of the lemon fruits. Strain.
2. Combine lemon juice with water, curry leaves, onion, chilli and salt.
3. Crush the onions and chilli with the back of spoon for a minute.
4. Chill and serve.

# Sambals
# & Salads

*"Sambal whips the tongue to greater activity, increases consumption and aids digestion. Without it a curry meal would not be complete."*

# Basic Mild Sambal

70 g grated coconut
Juice of ¼ small lime
½ small onion, sliced
1 green chilli, sliced
Salt to taste

### METHOD

1. Liquidise or grind coconut, chilli, onion and salt to a smooth paste.
2. Sprinkle lime juice. Serve with rice or bread.

# Basic Sambal For Beginners

2 red chillies, minced
30 g grated coconut or yogurt
3 medium sized tomatoes, sliced
Juice of ¼ small lime
½ small onion, sliced
Salt to taste

### METHOD

1. Combine tomatoes, coconut, onion, chillies and salt.
2. Sprinkle lime juice and mix well. Serve with rice or bread.

# Indonesian Ginger Sambal

10 red chillies, sliced
1 clove garlic, minced
1½ tsps minced ginger
Dash of vinegar

### METHOD

1. Liquidise or grind chillies, ginger and garlic. Moisten it with vinegar.

# Malay Shrimp Paste Sambal

4 cm piece shrimp paste, roasted
10 red chillies, sliced
Salt and lime juice to taste

### METHOD

1. Pound chillies, gradually adding shrimp paste and salt. The mixture should be neither too smooth nor too coarse.
2. Add lime juice before serving.

# Malay Dried Prawn Sambal

40 g dried prawns, roasted
¼ tsp shrimp paste, roasted
10 red chillies, sliced
Juice of lime/salt to taste

### METHOD

1. Pound together red chillies and salt.
2. Then add shrimp paste and dried prawns. Season with lime juice. The mixture should neither be too smooth nor too coarse.

# Indian Coriander Sambal

120 g coriander leaves or parsley
120 g grated coconut
¼ tsp asafoetida powder
1 tbsp oil
3 green chillies, sliced
1 tsp minced ginger
1 tsp mustard seeds
1½ tbsps lime juice
Salt to taste

### METHOD

1. Liquidise or grind the coriander leaves, chillies, ginger, salt and coconut to a smooth paste. Add lime juice.
2. Fry the mustard seeds until it splutters. Add asafoetida and pour mixture over the sambal.

# Mild Indian Sambal

125 g yellow split lentils, roasted
2 dried chillies, roasted
10 cloves garlic, sliced
Salt to taste

### METHOD

Combine lentils, chillies, garlic and salt and grind to a smooth paste.

# Indian Coconut Sambal

120 g grated coconut
3 green chillies, sliced
50 g coriander leaves
2 dried red chillies, broken
4 curry leaves
1 tsp lime juice or 1 tbsp curd
2 tbsps yellow split lentils, roasted, puffed
¼ tsp mustard seeds
2 tsps ghee
Salt to taste

METHOD

1. Grind or liquidise coconut, lentils, green chillies, coriander leaves, and salt to a smooth paste.
2. Fry mustard seeds, curry leaves and dried chillies and mix it with the paste. Add a teaspoon of lime juice or a tablespoon curd.

# Jaffna Curry Leaves Sambal

5 sprigs curry leaves
40 g grated coconut
4 green chillies, sliced
1 small onion, sliced
Lime juice and salt to taste

METHOD

1. Liquidise or grind coconut, curry leaves, chillies, onion and salt to a smooth paste.
2. Add lime juice before serving.

# Jaffna Mango Sambal

1 small raw mango, skinned, chopped
75 g grated coconut
1 curry leaf
5 green chillies
1 small onion, sliced
Salt to taste

METHOD

1. Liquidise or grind mango, coconut, curry leaf, chillies, onion and salt to a smooth paste.

# Jaffna Mint Sambal

40 g mint
30 g grated coconut
1 tsp ghee
4 dried chillies, each broken into two bits
1 small onion, sliced
Lime juice/salt to taste

METHOD

1. Heat ghee. Fry mint, coconut, chillies and onion lightly.
2. Then liquidise or grind it with salt to a smooth paste.
3. Add lime juice before serving.

# Indian Cucumber Sambal

1 medium sized cucumber
3 green chillies, shredded
1 tbsp mint, chopped
125 ml yogurt
3 small onions, shredded
1 small tomato, minced
1 tbsp coriander leaves, chopped
Salt to taste

METHOD

1. Skin and remove the seeds and then shred the cucumber. Rub with salt.
2. Now squeeze the cucumber to remove excess water and combine it with yogurt, onions, chillies, mint, coriander leaves, tomato and salt to taste. Serve at once.

**Note:**
This sambal is good with hot curries and mutton biriani.

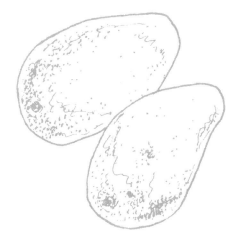

# Indian Onion Sambal

125 g onions, shredded
 3 green chillies, shredded
 1 tbsp coriander leaves, chopped
 75 g grated coconut
250 ml yogurt
Salt to taste

---

METHOD

1.  Rub a little salt (½ tsp) into onions and leave it to stand for 15 minutes.
2.  Just before serving, squeeze the onions to remove excess water and combine with chillies, coconut, coriander leaves, yogurt and salt.

Note:
This sambal is good with hot curries.

# Apple Sambal

1 apple, grated
1 cucumber, grated
1 clove garlic, grated
2 red chillies, minced
1 small onion, grated
70 ml vinegar

---

METHOD

1.  Sprinkle salt over apple, cucumber, onion and garlic and allow to stand for 15 minutes. Then squeeze out the excess liquid.
2.  Combine with vinegar and chillies.

# Jaffna Eggplant Sambal

1 large eggplant
1 red chilli, minced
1 green chilli, minced
2 small onions, minced
1 tbsp yogurt
2 tbsps coconut milk, thick
1 tbsp coriander leaves, chopped
Salt to taste

---

METHOD

1.  Bake the eggplant in the oven or under the grill or hot coals until the skins are blistered and nearly black. Scoop out the pulp.
2.  Mash the pulp and combine with onion, chillies, coriander leaves, coconut milk, yogurt and salt to taste.
3.  Serve with vegetarian dishes.

# Jaffna Mixed Sambal

1 medium sized cucumber
2 medium sized tomatoes
1 small carrot
1 large onion
1 green chilli, minced
2 red chillies, minced
5 tbsps coconut milk, thick
4 tbsps yogurt
1 tbsp coriander leaves
¼ tsp mustard seeds, roasted
Salt to taste

---

METHOD

1.  Slice the cucumber, onion and tomatoes very thinly.
2.  Skin and grate the carrot, and combine with cucumber, tomatoes, onion, chillies, coriander leaves, coconut milk, yogurt and salt. Sprinkle with mustard seeds.
3.  Serve with grilled chicken.

# Jaffna Beetroot Sambal

1 medium sized beetroot, boiled
2 small onions, minced
2 green chillies, minced
3 tbsps yogurt
1 tbsp coriander leaves, chopped
Salt to taste

METHOD
1. Peel the beetroot and cut into small bite-size pieces.
2. Put on a plate and combine with chillies, onion, coriander leaves, yogurt and salt.

# Sinhalese Maldive Fish Sambal

150 g maldive fish, pounded
450 g small onions
120 ml coconut milk, thick
120 ml coconut milk, thin
 50 g tamarind pulp
  1 sprig curry leaves
  3 cardamom pods, crushed
  2 tsps sugar
  1 tbsp chilli powder
  2 slices ginger, chopped
  3 cloves garlic, chopped
  4 cloves
  5 cm stick cinnamon
Oil
Salt to taste

METHOD
1. Slice onions very thinly and dry for a minute.
2. Heat oil and when hot, add onions, garlic and ginger until brown. Remove the excess oil leaving two table-spoonsful.
3. Now combine tamarind with thin coconut milk, chilli powder, maldive fish, curry leaves, cardamom pods, cloves, cinnamon and add to the fried ingredients. Mix well, and allow to simmer for 45 minutes.
4. Add sugar and thick coconut milk just before removing pan from the fire. Add salt. Stir.

# Malay Dried Whitebait Sambal

 90 g dried whitebait, cleaned
180 ml coconut milk, thick
 60 ml tamarind water
  1 stalk lemon grass, sliced
  1 small onion, sliced
 ¼ tsp shrimp paste
  1 tsp galangal powder
  4 candlenuts
  7 dried chillies
Oil
Salt to taste

METHOD
1 Liquidise candlenuts, chillies, onion, galangal powder, shrimp paste, lemon grass and a little oil to keep the mixture moving in the liquidiser.
2. Heat pan, add liquidised or ground ingredients and cook until brown.
3. Now add coconut milk, tamarind water and salt and let the gravy bubble.
4. In the meantime, deep fry the whitebait. Drain.
5. Add whitebait to gravy. When the oil comes to the surface, cook for a minute.

# Sri Lankan Fish Sambal

225 g cooked fish
  2 red chillies, minced
  1 cm piece ginger, minced
Pinch of mustard seeds, roasted
  1 large onion, minced
  2 green chillies, minced
  1 tbsp mint, chopped
Lemon juice and salt to taste

METHOD
1. Remove bones from fish and mash.
2. Combine with chillies, ginger, mustard seeds, onion, mint and salt. Sprinkle with lemon juice.
3. Serve with bread or plain rice.

# Sri Lankan Maldive Fish Sambal

16 g maldive fish
56 g dried chillies
56 g onions
Lime juice and salt to taste

METHOD
1. Liquidise or grind all the ingredients to a coarse paste.
2. Add lime juice and salt to taste.

# Straits Chinese Chicken Sambal

350 g chicken, cut into bite size pieces
25 dried chillies, pounded
13 small onions, pounded
7 candlenuts, pounded
Juice of a small lime
½ tsp monosodium glutamate
6 tbsps oil
4 tbsps light soya sauce
Sugar and salt to taste

METHOD

1. Marinate chicken in light soya sauce for 15 minutes.
2. Heat oil, fry chicken until brown, stirring briskly and remove.
3. Now stir in the pounded ingredients and fry till fragrant.
4. Add lime juice, sugar, salt, monosodium glutamate and chicken, stirring well to mix.
5. Dish onto a heatproof dish and steam in a steamer until meat is cooked.

# Straits Chinese Pork Sambal

450 g pork, de-boned, thinly sliced
5 small onions, minced
4 cloves garlic, minced
35 g oil
30 g lard
¼ tsp shrimp paste
1 tbsp fennel seeds, ground
13 dried chillies, ground
5 cm stick cinnamon
Juice of a small lemon
Salt to taste

METHOD

1. Squeeze out the juice of onion and garlic.
2. Heat oil and lard and fry the onion and garlic. Gradually add chillies, fennel paste, shrimp paste and fry until dark brown.
3. Add meat, cinnamon, salt and a little water. Stir, and let it simmer uncovered for about 15 – 18 minutes.
4. Add lemon juice, stir and serve.

*Straits Chinese Chicken Sambal.*

# Indonesian Chicken Sambal

1 kg chicken, de-boned
1 large onion, ground
4 cm piece lemon grass, ground
2 cm pieces galangal, ground
2 tbsps oil
1 tsp cumin seeds, ground
125 ml coconut milk, thick
6 red chillies, ground
3 cloves garlic, ground
2 cm piece fresh ginger, ground
1 tbsp coriander seeds, ground
1 tbsp lemon juice
1½ tbsps tamarind pulp

---

METHOD

1. Cut chicken into narrow strips and rub with tamarind pulp dissolved in two tablespoons of salted water.
2. Combine all ground ingredients with lemon juice.
3. Saute chicken in heated oil until brown. Add more oil if necessary.
4. Add spice mixture and coconut milk and allow to simmer until dry.

# Indonesian Egg and Prawn Sambal

350 g prawns, shelled
13 hard-boiled quail eggs, shelled
2 red chillies, sliced
2 green chillies, sliced
160 ml coconut milk
1 tsp sugar
1 tsp shrimp paste, roasted, and ground
2 slices galangal, ground
3 cloves garlic, ground
4 candlenuts, ground
7 small onions, ground
15 dried chillies, ground
6 tbsps oil
Salt to taste

---

METHOD

1. Heat oil, fry ground ingredients till fragrant.
2. Add prawns, chillies and stir fry until partially cooked.
3. Add salt, coconut milk, eggs and sugar. Simmer, stirring occasionally. Remove when all the ingredients are well blended and thick.

# Indonesian Chicken Sambal (2)

450 g chicken, de-boned, ½ cm cubed
250 ml coconut milk
1 curry leaf or bay leaf
1 tsp ground ginger
1 tsp shrimp paste, roasted, ground
5 small onions, ground
4 cloves garlic, ground
4 tbsps chilli paste
2 tbsps lemon juice
5 tbsps oil
Salt to taste

---

METHOD

1. Simmer chicken in coconut milk with a pinch of salt until partially done. Meanwhile combine ground ingredients, salt and lemon juice and pound.
2. Heat oil, saute ground ingredients lightly, stirring occasionally to make sure it does not burn. Add curry leaf.
3. Add chicken mixture and simmer until dry and done.

# Indonesian Meat Sambal

350 g meat, cut into 2 cm cubes
5 small onions, ground
5 cloves garlic, ground
50 ml coconut milk, thick
3 red chillies, sliced
3 tbsps peanut oil
½ tbsp coconut oil
1 tsp palm sugar
1 tsp shrimp paste, roasted
1½ tbsps chilli paste
1 tsp turmeric powder
1 tsp galangal powder
1 tbsp lemon juice
1 tsp salt

---

METHOD

1. Pound onions, garlic, palm sugar, shrimp paste, chilli paste, turmeric powder, galangal powder and salt.
2. Blend coconut oil and peanut oil and saute the pounded ingredients over a medium heat until fragrant.
3. Add meat, chillies, lemon juice, coconut milk and stir to mix well. Allow to simmer, stirring occasionally, until the meat is done or the oil appears on the surface.

# Indonesian Meat and Prawn Sambal

350 g meat, sliced thinly
350 g prawns, shelled, de-veined
175 g small onions, sliced
 13 red chillies, pounded coarsely
150 ml coconut milk
  1 tbsp tamarind water, thick
  1 tsp shrimp paste, roasted, pounded coarsely
  1 tsp salt
Oil
 50 ml water

### METHOD

1. Boil meat in 50 ml water and drain.
2. Heat a little oil, fry onions, meat and prawns separately. Keep aside.
3. Heat three tablespoons oil, fry the pounded chillies and shrimp paste until fragrant.
4. Add in coconut milk, tamarind water, fried ingredients and salt. Bring to the boil and cook, stirring occasionally, till the mixture is dry and oily.
5. Serve with white rice or plain pilau rice.

# Indonesian Macadamia Sambal

 13 macadamia nuts or candlenuts
  5 small onions, ground
  6 cloves garlic, ground
  9 red chillies, ground
2½ tbsps oil
200 ml coconut milk, thick
  1 tbsp palm sugar
1¼ tsp shrimp paste, roasted, ground
  1 tbsp galangal powder
  1 tbsp lemon juice
 ½ tsp salt

### METHOD

1. Pound candlenuts, onions, garlic, chillies, palm sugar, shrimp paste, salt, galangal powder and lemon juice.
2. Saute the pounded ingredients, stirring constantly to make sure that the mixture does not burn.
3. Add coconut milk and allow to simmer over a very low fire until the oil appears on the surface.

Note:
This sambal can be stored in jars for a month. When needed saute desired quantity in a little oil.

# Indonesian Fish Sambal

1¼ kg Spanish mackerel
750 ml coconut milk, thick
  3 lemon leaves
  1 stalk lemon grass, sliced
 13 red chillies, ground
 15 small onions, ground
  7 candlenuts, ground
  2 tsps sugar
  2 slices galangal, ground
  4 garlic pods, ground
  2 cm piece turmeric, ground
  2 cm piece dry ginger root, ground
  3 tbsps coriander seeds
Tamarind juice/salt to taste

### METHOD

1. Steam, de-bone and pound the fish finely.
2. Combine all the ingredients together and cook over a very low heat until the ingredients are very dry and golden brown. Stir occasionally and when dry, remove, cool and store in air tight jars.

# Mint Sambal

450 g dehydrated mint
112 g yellow split lentils
112 g dried chillies
  1 tbsp tamarind water
  1 tsp mustard seeds
  1 tbsp oil
  1 tbsp salt
 ¼ tsp asafoetida

### METHOD

1. Fry lentils and chillies until lentils are golden brown. Add salt.
2. Saute mustard seeds and asafoetida in a little oil and keep aside.
3. Liquidise or grind lentils, chillies and salt.
4. Roast mint on a dry pan for a few minutes. Add to the lentil mixture and grind or liquidise again.
5. Add tamarind water just before removing the ingredients from the liquidiser.
6. Remove the ground ingredients and mix with the mustard seeds and asafoetida.

Note:
This will keep for a month under refrigeration.

# Indian Red Pepper

13 dried chillies
112 g yellow split lentils
112 g black lentils
1 tbsp oil
1 tsp asafoetida
2 tbsps salt

### METHOD

1. Heat oil, fry lentils, chillies and asafoetida until brown.
2. Add salt, stir and remove to cool.
3. Liquidise or grind to a coarse powder.

### Note:

This will keep well for 2 weeks if stored in an air tight container. It can be a side dish for Indian pancakes or tossed over salads and Indian cottage cheese. When serving red pepper, stir in a little melted ghee.

# Singaporean Bean Curd Cake Salad

10 soya bean curd cakes, fried crisply, sliced
225 g beansprouts, blanched
2 cucumbers, shredded
2 red chillies, de-seeded, julienne
Sauce (see page 19)

### METHOD

1. Arrange the fried bean curd cakes on a plate. Top with beansprouts and chillies
2. Serve with sauce.

# Singaporean Vegetables and Fruit Salad

225 g beansprouts, blanched
175 g watercress, boiled, chopped
1 yam bean, shredded
125 g sliced pineapple, cubed
2 cucumbers, shredded
10 yellow soya bean curd cakes, fried, sliced thinly
Sauce (see page 21)

### METHOD

Mix well the vegetables and fruit with sauce and serve on a plate.

# Basic Spiced Fruit Salad

500 g tinned pineapples
500 g tinned mandarin oranges
500 g tinned mangoes
2 medium sized bananas, sliced
2 pears, sliced
2 tsps chilli powder
½ tsp ground cloves
¼ tsp nutmeg
Dash of pepper

### METHOD

1. Combine the spices together.
2. Drain and reserve the fruit syrup. Mix the fruit and spices and add as much syrup as you wish and chill for at least 6 hours.

# Vegetable Salad

1 medium sized cucumber, roughly chopped
1 large red capsicum, sliced thinly
4 medium sized tomatoes, quartered
2 onions, sliced
3 green chillies, de-seeded
1 tbsp chilli sauce
100 ml olive oil
50 ml wine vinegar
Pinch of nutmeg

### METHOD

1. Combine chilli sauce, vinegar, olive oil and nutmeg.
2. Toss all the vegetables with the d essing. Chill for 2 hours and serve.

# Indonesian Mixed Fruit and Vegetable Salad

1 medium sized cucumber, sliced
1 apple, sliced thickly
½ medium sized pineapple, diced
1 mango, skinned, sliced
½ papaya, diced
½ tsp shrimp paste, baked in foil
1 tbsp palm sugar
1 tbsp lemon juice
1 tbsp chilli powder
½ tbsp Javanese soya sauce

## METHOD

1. Combine shrimp paste, palm sugar, lemon juice, chilli powder and soya sauce in a liquidiser for a minute.
2. Toss with the cucumber, apple, pineapple, mango, and papaya. Allow to stand for 20 minutes before serving.

# Indonesian Boiled Vegetable Salad

1 green cucumber, cut into thick strips
3 medium sized potatoes, boiled, sliced
1 small cabbage, blanched, shredded
100 g fresh beans, 2 cm lengths, lightly cooked
120 g beansprouts, blanched
2 hard boiled eggs, shelled, halved
4 bean curd cakes, deep fried, cubed
2 medium sized carrots, sliced lengthwise, lightly cooked
Vegetable sauce (see page 21)

## METHOD

1. Arrange the vegetables in layers on a flat plate in the following order. Potatoes, french beans, carrots, cabbage, bean curd cakes, cucumber, beansprouts, eggs.
2. Pour the sauce over.

*Indonesian Mixed Fruit and Vegetable Salad.*

# Hindu Salad

450 g green lentils
225 g grated coconut
225 g cucumber, shredded
  2 red chillies, sliced thinly
  2 green chillies, sliced thinly
  2 tbsps coriander leaves
  2 tbsps lime juice
  1 tbsp ghee
  1 tsp mustard seeds
  1 tsp salt

METHOD

1. Soak the lentils for 3 hours. Strain and put into a flat bowl.
2. Add cucumber, coconut, coriander leaves, salt and lime juice to the green lentils. Mix thoroughly.
3. Heat ghee, saute chillies, mustard seeds and add to the lentils. Serve.

Note:
According to the Ramayana, this was one of Lord Rama's favourite foods.

# Philippine Papaya Salad

  1 medium sized semi-ripe papaya
  1 medium lettuce
  3 green chillies, minced
  1 tbsp lemon juice
½ tsp grated ginger
Salt to taste

METHOD

1. Wash and separate the lettuce leaves and arrange on a flat plate.
2. Skin, de-seed and grate papaya coarsely and combine with ginger, chillies, lemon juice and salt. Serve on lettuce leaves.

# Thai Fruit and Prawn Salad

  1 large papaya, skinned, de-seeded, thinly sliced
  1 small cabbage, finely shredded
  2 medium sized tomatoes, sliced
  1 lettuce, washed, separated
225 g prawns, cooked, shelled
  2 green chillies, slivered
  2 red chillies, slivered
  2 spring onions, chopped
  3 mint leaves
  1 tbsp palm sugar
1½ tbsp fish sauce
  2 tbsp roasted peanuts, coarsely ground
¼ tbsp chilli powder (optional)
Juice of a lime

METHOD

1. Arrange the lettuce leaves on a shallow dish.
2. Now lay the cabbage, papaya and tomatoes mixed together on the lettuce leaves.
3. Sprinkle prawns and then peanuts and chillies.
4. Mix the lime juice, fish sauce, chilli powder, palm sugar, mint and spring onions until the sugar has dissolved.
5. Pour this dressing over the salad. Chill for 2 hours before serving.

# Indochinese Prawn and Pork Salad

450 g cooked prawns, shelled, diced
650 g cooked pork, cubed small
  2 medium sized cucumbers, skinned, sliced
  3 cloves garlic, minced
  4 mint leaves, chopped
  1 onion, thinly sliced
½ tsp ground coriander
1½ tsps freshly ground pepper
  3 tbsps vinegar
  2 tbsps lemon juice
½ tsp chilli powder
  1 tsp sugar
Salt to taste

METHOD

1. Combine coriander, pepper, chilli, sugar, vinegar, lemon juice, salt, garlic and leave for 10 minutes.
2. Combine with pork, prawns and cucumber. Toss lightly.
3. Sprinkle with mint leaves and onion.

# Malaysian Vegetable Salad

280 g beansprouts, boiled
150 g cabbage, boiled, shredded
150 g long beans, cut into 3 cm lengths, boiled
125 g cucumber, shredded
180 g grated coconut
125 g dried prawns, pounded fine
  2 wrinkled lime leaves
  5 soya bean cakes, fried whole and diced
½ tsp shrimp paste, roasted
  1 tsp garlic, ground
13 red chillies, pounded
  6 small onions, ground
  3 hard boiled eggs, shelled, halved
Salt to taste

---

METHOD

---

1. Pound coarsely prawns, shrimp paste, garlic, chillies, onions, wrinkled lime leaves and salt together for a minute or two.
2. Combine with the grated coconut and steam for 15 minutes.
3. Mix with the beansprouts, cabbage, long beans, cucumber, eggs and soya bean cakes.


# Straits Chinese Vegetable Salad

125 g beansprouts, cleaned, blanched lightly
125 g french beans, 3 cm lengths, boiled lightly
400 g tender spinach, 2 cm lengths, blanched lightly
225 g cabbage, shredded finely, blanched lightly
225 g potatoes, skinned, boiled, sliced
  7 hard boiled eggs, shelled, halved
  7 soya bean curd cakes, 1 cm cubes, deep fried
Sauce (see page 21)

---

METHOD

---

1. Arrange the french beans, spinach, cabbage, potatoes, bean sprouts, eggs and bean curd cakes in separate heaps on a large platter.
2. Serve with sauce.

# Chutneys
# & Pickles

*Chutneys and pickles are the 'Dining Whips' in the festive meal of India.*

# Basic Sweet Apple Chutney

1¼ kg sour apples
½ kg sugar
400 ml vinegar
125 g raisins
20 g ginger
15 g salt

### METHOD

1. Peel, core and slice apples and combine with raisins and ginger.
2. Combine salt and a little water and bring to a boil until apples become soft.
3. Add vinegar and sugar and continue to cook until a thick consistency is obtained. Bottle into jars while still hot.

# Basic Lime Pickle

30 limes
225 g salt
50 g chilli powder

### METHOD

1. Wash, dry and slit each lime fruit into four, without severing the pieces.
2. Mix salt and chilli powder and stuff into the lime fruits.
3. Put into jars and place them in the sun for four to five days. Allow it to stand for another fifteen days before serving.

# Sweet and Sour Mango Chutney

1¼ kg mango slices
1¼ kg sugar
70 g salt
450 ml vinegar
30 g red chillies
10 g cumin seeds
Water

### METHOD

1. Grind the chillies in a little vinegar.
2. Boil the mangoes in a little water. Then combine sugar, salt, vinegar, red chillies and cumin seeds. Bring to a boil.
3. Cook over a medium fire until a jam-like consistency is obtained.

# Sweet and Hot Apricot Chutney

1 kg dried apricots
700 g sugar
750 ml vinegar
30 g salt
30 g fresh ginger
25 g chillies, whole

### METHOD

1. Soak apricots for 2 – 3 days and then boil them until soft.
2. Liquidise or grind ginger, chillies, salt and sugar with a little vinegar and then mix thoroughly with the apricots.
3. Boil the mixture in the rest of the vinegar to a thick consistency. When cool, put the chutney into jars.

# Tamarind Chutney

450 g tamarind, seedless
450 g sugar
13 red chillies, ground
30 g chilli powder
500 ml vinegar
225 g raisins
63 g ginger, ground
6 cloves garlic, ground
2 tbsps salt

### METHOD

1. Grind all the chillies, garlic, ginger in vinegar.
2. Squeeze the tamarind in vinegar and strain through a cheesecloth.
3. Combine tamarind with sugar, salt, raisins, chilli powder and ground ingredients. Boil until the syrup is thick.

# Mint Chutney

75 g mint, chopped
3½ tbsps raisins
1 tsp salt
1 tsp chilli powder
3 tbsps sugar
vinegar

### METHOD

1. Rub the chilli powder and salt into the mint leaves. Then grind or liquidise to a paste with raisins and sugar.
2. Blend with vinegar, cool and jar.

# Tomato Chutney

　1 kg tomatoes
250 ml vinegar
　4 red chillies
　4 tbsps sugar
　1 tsp garlic paste
　2 tbsps ginger paste
　2 tbsps salt

---

METHOD

1. Blanch the tomatoes and remove the skins. Then cut into pieces.
2. Combine tomatoes, chillies, ginger and garlic with a little water and cook the tomatoes over a medium fire until pulpy.
3. Add salt and sugar until it has a glazed appearance.
4. Remove from the fire and add vinegar.

# Chilli Chutney

225 g green chillies
300 ml vinegar
1½ tbsps lime juice
　2 tbsps salt

---

METHOD

1. Slice chillies crosswise into 1 cm pieces. Add salt and allow to stand in the sun for 4 hours.
2. Bring vinegar, lime juice to a boil and then add chillies.
3. Put in a sterile jar and seal tightly.

# Prune Chutney

450 g dried prunes
120 g sugar
500 ml water
　1 medium sized lemon, juice and grate rind
　2 peppercorns, whole
　1 tsp cinnamon powder
　1 tsp allspice
　4 cloves
　2 tbsps vinegar

---

METHOD

1. Wash and soak prunes for 12 hours. Simmer in the same liquid until tender but do not overcook. Remove stones.
2. Now add to the liquid the grated rind, juice of lemon, vinegar, sugar, cinnamon powder, allspice, cloves and peppercorns. Simmer for 10 minutes.
3. Remove fruit into jars, boil down the syrup for another 5 minutes, pour over the prunes and seal jars.

# Indonesian Vegetable Pickle

　4 medium sized cucumbers
　1 medium sized carrot
　5 small onions, halved
　4 cloves garlic, chopped
200 ml vinegar
　65 ml water
　4 red chillies, whole
　1 tsp turmeric powder
　1 tbsp sugar
　1 tbsp fresh ginger, chopped
　2 tbsps ground candlenut
　3 tbsps salt
Oil

---

METHOD

1. Peel, cut cucumber lengthwise into finger-length pieces. Remove pulpy core. Similarly, skin and cut carrot.
2. Salt and chill them for 3 hours. Wash, squeeze out excess liquid and dry.
3. Saute onion, garlic, ginger in oil until soft.
4. Add ground candlenut, turmeric powder, sugar and a tablespoon of salt. Stir together, then add vinegar and water. Simmer for 10 minutes.
5. Pour this mixture over the cucumber, whole chillies and carrot. Let stand at least for 1 hour before serving.

# Indian Vegetable Pickle

1 kg carrot
1 kg cauliflower
½ kg turnip
125 g garlic
100 g mustard, ground coarsely
200 ml vinegar
60 g red chillies, whole
50 g garam masala
250 g palm sugar
125 g ginger
400 g salt
200 ml mustard oil

### METHOD

1. Peel and cut carrot and turnip into 1½ cm pieces and the cauliflower into small pieces. Soak in boiling wate for 1 minute. Drain. Keep dry for 12 hours.
2. Grind garlic, ginger each separately. Heat oil, fry the garlic, then add the ginger and fry until brown. Add whole chillies.
3. Boil the sugar with the vinegar until a syrup is formed. Remove.
4. Add mustard, garam masala, salt, oil, fried garlic, ginger, chillies and vegetables to syrup. Put in a jar and keep in the sun for 15 days. This pickle will keep for a year.

# Indian Chicken Pickle

1 kg chicken
125 ml mustard oil
125 g red chillies, paste
120 ml vinegar
120 g salt
1 tbsp fenugreek seeds paste
4 tbsps ginger paste
2 tbsps mustard seeds paste
2 tbsps turmeric paste
2 tbsps garlic paste

### METHOD

1. Grind the spices each separately into a paste with a little vinegar.
2. Cut the chicken into bite-size pieces (with the bones) and fry lightly.
3. Heat all the oil, fry the ginger, mustard, fenugreek seeds, garlic and chilli pastes. Add chicken and brown it in the spices. Add vinegar.
4. The chicken must be soaked in oil. When storing in jars, make sure the chicken is completely submerged in oil. Add salt.

# Indian Prawn Pickle

700 g prawns, shelled
200 ml vinegar
2 tbsps cumin seeds
¼ tsp mustard seeds, crushed
13 cloves garlic
1½ tbsps chilli paste
6 tbsps sesame oil
Salt to taste

### METHOD

1. Grind the garlic and cumin seeds into a paste with a little vinegar. Add mustard seeds.
2. Clean and dry prawns. Rub with salt and fry lightly in a little oil.
3. Heat the remaining oil and fry the paste combined with the chilli paste. When it becomes fragrant, add sesame oil, prawns and vinegar. Cook until the mixture is dry. Cool and then bottle.

# Indian Mango Pickle

1 kg green mangoes
300 ml groundnut oil
200 g mustard seeds, crushed
200 g salt
3¼ tbsp chilli powder
3½ tbsp turmeric powder
1½ tbsp asafoetida powder
150 g fenugreek seeds

### METHOD

1. Wash, dry mangoes and cut into small pieces. Rub with salt and turmeric powder and keep in a jar for 3 days.
2. Brown the fenugreek seeds in a little oil; then grind them finely.
3. Combine with asafoetida, mustard seeds, chilli powder and salt.
4. Add mango pieces and the rest of the oil and mix thoroughly. Fill in the jars. It will be ready after a week.

# Chinese Chilli Pickle

250 g green chillies, sliced finely in rounds
250 ml water
250 ml vinegar
2¼ tbsps sugar
2¼ tbsps salt

### METHOD

1. Boil together salt, sugar, vinegar and water. When boiling, remove from the fire and strain.
2. When cool, add sliced chillies.

# Indian Onion Pickle

1 kg small onions, quartered
120 g salt
10 ml mustard oil
½ tbsp mustard powder
4 tbsps chilli powder

### METHOD

1. Slit the onions without severing them. Add 60 g salt and then wash off after 3 hours. Dry.
2. Mix the mustard powder, oil, chilli powder, and salt. Stuff the onions with this mixture and put them in a jar.
3. Cover with water. Keep the jar in the sun for 4 – 5 days.

# Sri Lankan Fish Pickle

450 g white fish slices
250 ml vinegar
1 tbsp tamarind pulp
1¼ tbsps salt
2¼ tsps coriander powder
1¼ tbsps sugar
1¼ tbsps chilli powder
1 tbsp turmeric powder
Oil for frying

### METHOD

1. Cut, dry fish and rub with turmeric powder and salt; deep fry.
2. Soak tamarind pulp in vinegar and combine with the coriander powder, chilli powder, sugar and bring to a boil. Adjust seasoning.
3. Add fried fish slices and remove. Allow to cool; then store in earthenware jars.

# Thai Vegetable Pickle

225 g cauliflower
76 g cucumber, skinned, seeded
125 g corn kernels
100 g cabbage, shredded
550 ml rice wine
140 ml peanut oil
1 tbsp sesame seeds
1 tbsp sugar
1 tbsp garlic paste
2 tbsp red chilli paste
2½ tbsps onion paste
1¼ tsps salt

### METHOD

1. Break cauliflower into small sprigs; cube the cucumber and strip corn off cob.
2. Heat the wine, sugar and salt until boiling. Immerse the vegetables and cook until tender but do not overcook them. Remove and set aside.
3. Heat the oil, fry the paste ingredients until brown.
4. Add vegetables and wine mixture and stir for two minutes.
5. Pour into a serving dish and sprinkle with sesame seeds. Leave to cool and pour into a jar, cover tightly and chill.

# Indonesian Pork Pickle

225 g pork, cut into 1 cm cubes
250 ml broth
4 candlenuts, ground
1 tbsp oil
5 tbsps rice vinegar
1 tbsp lime juice
1 tsp garlic, ground
1 tsp ground ginger
½ tsp turmeric, ground
½ tsp pepper
1 tsp salt
½ tsp sugar
½ tsp mustard powder

### METHOD

1. Simmer pork cubes in broth with salt for 12 minutes. Drain, reserving 2 tablespoons of the broth.
2. Combine garlic, ginger, turmeric, candlenuts, salt and pepper.
3. Saute these ingredients until brown. Add vinegar, lime juice, sugar and mustard and stir for 2 minutes.
4. Add pork cubes with two tablespoons broth and cook for 2 minutes. Cool and bottle.

# Accompaniments

*"Accompaniments or side dishes, like the tributaries of the river, feed the mainstream. They add zest to any meal."*
— *Hindu saying*

# Thai Beans

½ kg dried lima beans
Peanut oil
Salt to taste

## METHOD

1. Soak dried lima beans overnight. Drain and dry them.
2. Fry in heated oil. Drain. Sprinkle with salt.

Note:
Papadoms/krupuk — (see page vii)

# Thai Corn Crisps

12 ears of corn
250 ml coconut milk
Salt to taste

## METHOD

1. Remove the husks and silks of corn.
2. Dilute coconut milk and add salt.
3. Roast the corn over charcoal fire, dipping in salted dilution until the corn is well roasted.

# Indonesian Spicy Coconut Balls

250 g freshly grated coconut
2 cloves garlic, minced
3 eggs
1 tbsp flour
½ tsp turmeric powder
½ tsp galangal powder
½ tsp lemon grass powder
½ tsp coriander powder
¼ tsp sugar
½ tsp shrimp paste, roasted, pounded
1 tsp salt
Oil

## METHOD

1. Combine coconut, garlic, turmeric powder, galangal powder, lemon grass powder, coriander powder, sugar, shrimp paste, salt, flour and eggs.
2. Make into small balls and deep fry until golden brown.
3. Coconut balls may be used as a garnish for fried rice.

# Indonesian Peanut Fritters

175 g rice flour
125 g roasted peanuts
½ tsp turmeric powder
2 cloves garlic, crushed
1 tsp ground ginger
½ tsp chilli powder
1 tsp coriander powder
Oil
Salt to taste
Water

## METHOD

1. Combine egg, salt, chilli powder and coriander powder.
2. Add rice flour and enough water to make a batter which flows from a spoon smoothly.
3. Now combine with garlic, ginger, turmeric powder and stir continuously adding the peanuts.
4. Heat oil, fry a tablespoon of batter until it turns brown.
5. Drain on absorbent paper.

# Indonesian Coconut-Peanut Garnish

250 g grated coconut
125 g roasted peanuts
1 small onion, minced
2 cloves garlic, crushed, chopped
2 cm piece ginger, crushed
½ tsp coriander powder
1 tsp cumin powder
1 tbsp tamarind water
2¼ tsps brown sugar
1 tbsp vegetable oil

## METHOD

1. Combine together coconut, cumin, coriander, onion, garlic, ginger, sugar and tamarind water.
2. Smear oil in a pan and fry the mixture over a very low heat, stirring all the time, until it is golden and crisp.
3. Allow to cool, mix in the roasted peanuts, and serve.

# Indonesian Peanuts

125 g peanuts, raw
Salt to taste

---

METHOD

1. Dry-fry the peanuts in a heavy pan until they are cooked.
2. Sprinkle salt and stir for a minute, remove.

# Malay Fried Whitebait and Peanuts

200 g dried whitebait, cleaned
50 g roasted peanuts
3 tsps vinegar
3 tbsps chilli paste
2½ tsps sugar
Salt to taste
Oil

---

METHOD

1. Deep fry whitebait until crisp and brown. Drain.
2. Heat ten tablespoons oil, add chilli paste and fry for two minutes.
3. Then add sugar and salt and fry for another two minutes.
4. Add vinegar and when the mixture begins to thicken, add fried whitebait and peanuts. Stir well and then drain off excess oil.

# Chinese Prawn Crisps

450 g king-sized prawns
1 egg
½ tsp pepper
65 g cornflour
2½ tbsps water
Salt to taste
Oil

---

METHOD

1. Shell and de-vein the prawns, leaving the tails intact.
2. Combine sieved cornflour, salt, pepper with egg yolk and water.
3. Beat slowly and leave it aside for 15 – 20 minutes.
4. Whisk egg white briskly and fold into the flour mixture, making a smooth thick batter.
5. Heat oil, dip each prawn by its tail into the batter and deep fry until golden brown and crisp. Drain.

# Jaffna Preserved Green Chillies

1 kg green chillies
1¼ litres curd
225 g salt

---

METHOD

1. Remove stalks and slit the chillies at the tips.
2. Dissolve the salt in the curd.
3. Soak the chillies in the curd mixture for 3 – 4 days, stirring it once every day.
4. Take the chillies from the curds and keep them out in the sun. Then put the chillies back into the curd mixture.
5. Repeat this process until they become crisp.
6. Store in a container and, when required, fry in oil until brown and crisp.

# Indian Preserved Potato Chips

1 kg potatoes
Water
Salt to taste

---

METHOD

1. Boil the potatoes partially with salt to taste.
2. Cut into thin rounds and dry them out in the sun until crisp.
3. Store in air tight tins and use when required.

# Indian Vegetable Wafers

½ kg bitter gourds
1 tsp chilli powder
Salt to taste

---

METHOD

1. Slice the bitter gourds thinly.
2. Mix them with chilli powder and salt and dry in the sun until crisp.
3. Store in air tight containers and fry when required until crisp and brown.

# Indian Fried Green Chillies

Green chillies
Salt
Garlic
Oil

METHOD

1. Slit green chillies.
2. Take equal quantities by weight of garlic and salt. Pound well.
3. Stuff the green chillies with this mixture.
4. Deep fry.

# Indian Potato Straws

1 large potato
1 tsp caraway seeds
½ tsp chilli powder
½ tsp salt

METHOD

1. Grate potato, wash, drain and dry in cloth.
2. Deep fry to golden brown.
3. Drain oil and mix with salt, caraway seeds and chilli powder.

# Caribbean Indian Banana Chips

2 unripe bananas
Oil
Salt

METHOD

1. Slice the bananas into thin slices.
2. Smear salt and leave it aside for 10 minutes. Then drain.
3. Heat oil, deep fry. Drain, cool and store in an air tight container.

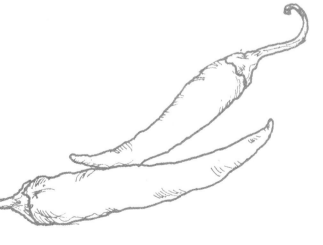

# INDEX

**Notes**

# Notes

**Notes**